"I wish when I was a teen, I had someone like Noah as a peer. I was a workaholic without great personal time management skills. I succeeded at a lot but wasn't organized in my passions or drivenness, so it created a lot of confusion. I love that quote that says, 'Work smarter, not harder.' Along comes Noah who has the ability to articulate and put together a track of mentoring for you that might just change your life. This book would be excellent for youth organizations to go through as a workbook or for youth groups to raise up leaders with. It fills a huge void when it comes to emotionally intelligent books for young men and women who have greatness inside and want to intentionally express it. Buy this if you want to get started in a powerful way right out of the gate of your teenage years."
—**SHAWN BOLZ**, Author, Speaker, and TV Personality
www.bolzministries.com

"Fascinating and practical, inspiring and groundbreaking, *Trailblazing Your Teen Years* is a book written for such a time as this. Never before have teens and young adults faced such challenges. Noah Halloran has written a game-changer to help move you past life's obstacles and not only survive, but thrive. A must-read for not only teens but adults."
—**LAURA FRANTZ**, Christy Award-winning author
of *An Uncommon Woman*

"As a Motivational Speaker I have had the unique privilege of ministering into the youth culture of over 100 nations. I can wholeheartedly say that if each teenager I have taught were to read Noah Halloran's book, *Trailblazing Your Teen Years*, and practice its principles, a revolutionary movement of youth influencers would erupt around the world. All the essentials for a life of eternal impact are simply spelled throughout the pages of his book with practical application and resources included. Halloran artfully weaves Biblical truths, personal stories, and those from the lives of history-makers in a way that will challenge and provoke readers of all ages. However, let me warn you that what Halloran presents doesn't fit into the genre of much of the narcissistic Christian literature of this day. If you are merely looking for an entertaining read that makes you feel good about yourself this is not the book for you. But if you yearn for dynamic change in your life that will transform not only you but also the desperately needy world around you then this book— which is more like a very practical spiritual journey— you will want to begin as soon as possible!"

—**JEFF PRATT**, Founder and Spiritual Director of Axiom Monastic Communities, and author of *The Homeward Call: A Contemplative Journey Into A Love That Will Not Let You Go*

"I wish I had a guy like Noah around when I was in high school and college, who had challenged me to think through these foundational issues of identity, discipline, balance, addictions, habits, taking thoughts captive, and living your one and only life with purpose. Noah has a great way of laying out the challenge and calling us UP, using a delicate balance of inviting us to discover who we really are, AND challenging us to live fully into that potential. Perhaps written for teens, there are many life lessons for all of us contained in these pages! Tackle these things now, and there will be nothing that can stop you from being everything you were created to be!"

—**MELISSA CHEESEMAN ROGERS**, Physician, Speaker, and Co-Founder of Wellspring Prayer Center

"Noah is speaking to a generation that has been fed the lie that freedom comes only from individual expression and self-fulfillment. As a teacher, I see the youth struggle daily to use their attire, speech, and actions to obtain these illusions society preaches as truth. Why do we now have a greater percentage of youth searching for their identity, yet more than ever we see them coming up empty? In *Trailblazing Your Teen Years,* Noah has provided a map to the true freedom that comes from surrendering ourselves to the one and only God. *"It is for freedom that Christ has set us free. Stand firm, then, and do not let yourselves be burdened again by a yoke of slavery"* (Galatians 5:1, NIV). We've become slaves to the need for self-expression, individuality, and personal fulfillment. In its most simple form, Noah speaks the basic truth of life. The one choice we truly have to make in our life is to choose love. In that choice, God frees us from the slavery of sin and the masquerade of earthly treasures it promotes. If our youth can listen to the words Noah is giving them, then they can truly be the generation that finally finds what so many have struggled for: freedom, peace, and joy that can only be found in Christ."

—**ADAM REID**, Child of Christ, Father, Teacher, and
Ministry Leader for Fellowship of Christian Athletes

"Trailblazing Your Teen Years is applicable to all ages. Noah doesn't just write inspiring words for teenagers. He walks out what he preaches by taking a leap of faith and uses the gift God gave him in writing with boldness and calling all of us higher. I'm taking each piece of gold hidden within his writing and using it to propel me further along in my own destiny as God's treasured possession."

—**CARMEN EBY**, Missionary and Blogger of *Grace for That*

"Trailblazing Your Teen Years is a must-read book for any person, teen or adult, looking to succeed in life. Not only is Noah's teaching practical, it's spiritually uplifting."

—**CRYSTAL CAUDILL**, Mom of Teenage Boys and
Speaker for Teenage Writers

Trailblazing
Your Teen
Years

TRAILBLAZING YOUR TEEN YEARS

Successful Habits to
LAUNCH out of the norms,
LEAD ahead of the pack, and
LAND into your destiny

NOAH HALLORAN

Printed in the United States of America

Published by Author Academy Elite
PO Box 43, Powell, OH 43035
www.AuthorAcademyElite.com

Library of Congress Control Number: 2020902793

ISBN: 978-1-64746-144-7 (paperback)
ISBN: 978-1-64746-145-4 (hardback)
ISBN: 978-1-64746-146-1 (ebook)

Available in paperback, hardback, e-book, and audiobook

Unless otherwise noted, Scripture quotations are taken from the New American Standard Bible˚, NASB. © 1960, 1962, 1963, 1968, 1971, 1972, 1973, 1975, 1977, 1995 by the Lockman Foundation. Used by permission. All rights reserved.

Scripture quotations marked (NIV) are taken from the Holy Bible, New International Version®. © 1973, 1978, 1984, 2011 by Biblica, Inc.TM. Used by permission of Zondervan. All rights reserved worldwide.

Scripture quotations marked (NLT) are taken from the Holy Bible, New Living Translation˚. © 1996, 2004, 2015 by Tyndale House Foundation. Used by permission of Tyndale House Publishers, Inc. Carol Stream, IL 60188. All rights reserved.

Scripture quotations marked (TPT) are taken from The Passion Translation˚. © 2017, 2018 by Passion and Fire Ministries, Inc. Used by permission. All rights reserved.

Scripture quotations marked (ESV) are taken from the Holy Bible, English Standard Version˚. © 2001 by Crossway, a publishing ministry of Good News Publishers. Used by permission. All rights reserved.

Scripture quotations marked (NKJV) are taken from New King James Version˚. Copyright © 1982 by Thomas Nelson. Used by permission. All rights reserved.

Any Internet addresses (websites, blogs, etc.) and telephone numbers printed in this book are offered as a resource. They are not intended in any way to be or imply an endorsement by Author Academy Elite or the author, nor does Author Academy Elite or the author vouch for the content of these sites and numbers for the life of this book.

I dedicate this book to all the teenagers
trying to find their place in this world.
May you trailblaze your own path to success.

"Do not go where the path may lead,
go instead where there is no path and leave a trail."
—Ralph W. Emerson

CONTENTS

PART 1: LAUNCH

PART 2: LEAD

PART 3: LAND

BONUS

APPENDICES

PART 1:

LAUNCH

$\longrightarrow$

This is Your Captain Speaking:
Fasten Your Seatbelts and Prepare for Take Off

You'll be on your way up!
You'll be seeing great sights!
You'll join the highfliers
Who soar to high heights.
—Dr. Seuss

1

FORMING HABITS

*D*o you have a hard time juggling school, home, and extra-curricular activities?

    Do you get stressed when planning for your future?

Do you desire to live a productive, happy, relaxing, and fulfilling life?

Most teens, including myself, answered yes to at least one of these questions. No doubt about it, the teen years are hard. Sadly, most of us have no clue about how to deal with life's tough issues. It's easy to become overwhelmed and discouraged.

Think about it. How can we be expected to know how to change a tire, what step comes next in the Krebs Cycle, and how to differentiate the five hundred King Henry's of European History? We're supposed to manage all this and maintain our cool with fluctuating hormones, school crushes, and the competition. Seriously, this stuff is not easy.

Therefore, it's crucial to establish good habits as early as possible. Setting good habits today sets us up for success tomorrow. Repetition forms habits and helps us conserve energy by not requiring a ton of brain power for every decision we make. Once a habit is set, it's practiced unconsciously over and over.

Do you have to put a reminder on your phone to brush your teeth every day? Probably not, because it's a habit. What about social media? Do you habitually compare yourself to others while scrolling through Instagram? There are many things we do subconsciously, and we don't even realize we're doing it.

This book focuses on breaking unhealthy habits and replacing them with healthy ones so we can progress from mediocre to exceptional. You'll discover each chapter will address an area where teens may struggle. I hope you don't feel like you need to conquer all these habits immediately—that would be unrealistic and would leave you frustrated. However, if you find one you want to tackle first and place your focus there, then you can move on to the next when you're ready. This way, you can measure your growth and focus on one aspect at a time.

When I establish a habit, I like to use the 21/90 rule. This rule says it takes twenty-one days to create a habit and ninety days to create a lifestyle. It's as straightforward as it sounds. You commit to pursuing a goal for twenty-one days. After twenty-one days, this goal should become part of your routine. As you continue to incorporate it into your routine for ninety more days, then that which you started on purpose now becomes automatic. Now, it's more than a habit—it's part of your lifestyle.

Take dieting, for example. The first week may be hard, but by twenty-one days, you've probably established some pretty good eating habits. By extending this for ninety more days, you're no longer dieting, but instead, living healthy and seeing much success!

What I want for you is to live victoriously. You'll be amazed at your accomplishments by tackling one goal at a time, and you'll begin achieving things you never imagined were possible. I know this firsthand from measuring my personal growth in character, school, and athletics. Keep in mind, everything big starts small. When you focus on the next step, it prevents the sensations of feeling overwhelmed and discouraged.

But no pressure. We all need to understand it's okay not to have everything figured out or in order. Life is messy, and many of us tend to hide this fact instead of opening-up as our authentic selves. Why are we so afraid to show the world who we really are? The world craves real people. We need the authentic you to show up filled up so you can pour out your God-given gifts and talents.

I encourage you not to fall into the imitation trap. Don't try to mimic anyone around you, but instead, discover who you are and be true to yourself. You'll be the happiest when you live your life according to God's design, not how people around you want you to live it.

Don't get discouraged if you don't know your authentic self yet. As we journey through this book, I'll ask some deep questions that will require you to pause and ponder. Your answers will help reveal who God created you to be by helping you discover dreams He's placed in your heart, issues that continually draw your attention, and places you want to influence. Honestly, this process can take a lifetime to figure out. The more we know our Maker, the more we will know ourselves.

You'll notice I discuss the importance of faith and how everything we do should stem from our core beliefs. Feelings change, but God never changes. God needs to be at the center of our lives, especially in teen years, because emotions are a roller coaster. They're unreliable and can't be trusted. The good news is when we're rooted in God, we're less likely to succumb to our emotions and every rise of hormone rage—if you know what I mean.

I'm not going to lie by saying the teen years will be sunshine and rainbows or unicorns and kittens if you simply follow seven easy steps, as many self-help books suggest. I wish it were that easy. But life is what we make it. I'll teach you how to roll with the punches and dust yourself off after a fall.

We're all works in progress. Embracing our shortcomings shows authenticity that will attract the respect of others. When we understand this, the teen years can be full of fun, healthy relationships, new things, and great memories.

It's also important to know no matter how independent we are, we can't go it alone. Not only do we need to think for ourselves and go after our goals, we also need to find positive influences in our lives. I've had parents, teachers, and coaches who've guided me to reach farther, push harder, and dream bigger than I ever had imagined. I encourage you to find people in your life who'll support you along the way. I know I wouldn't be where I am today without help from others.

In fact, to support and encourage you is why I'm so passionate about this book!

I write this book as your friend and someone who wants what's best for you. I'll share with you what's worked for me and what hasn't. Amidst these pages, we'll navigate life together. I'm no expert, not in the slightest, but I hope to guide you on your road to success. I'll point out the caution signs, prepare you for the slippery-when-wet signs, and encourage you when to stay your course. As we journey together, you'll find the confidence and assurance you'll need to arrive at your God-appointed destiny with limited delays and maximum enjoyment.

You'll learn how to become a confident decision-maker, an independent thinker, and an original pathfinder. You'll discover secrets to succeeding in school and balancing all life throws at you. You'll learn how to push past the difficulties and persevere, even in the face of failure.

So, if I'm going to be your tour guide, let me tell you a little about myself. I'm a sixteen-year-old junior in high school and have a passion for helping others my age. Despite having a more reserved personality, I consider myself friendly. When I joined the track team in sixth grade, I discovered my love for distance running. I lettered in cross country my eighth-grade year and won my age group in a half marathon in 2017. Because I run a lot, you'll notice I like to use running analogies. It's amazing how you can apply running to practically everything.

My family is a blessing. I have a great mom and dad and one brother, five years younger than me. Although I've always been a pretty good student, I was unorganized in elementary school. My dad used to take me back to school nearly every day so I could retrieve my forgotten homework from my locker. The janitors would have to let us in because the doors were already locked. It was so embarrassing.

Luckily, I soon discovered ways to dramatically improve my organization and the quality of my studying. As a result, my class rank gradually increased to ninth in a class of 513 students in my sophomore year. Humbly, I did this by spending minimal time studying outside of the classroom, which reduced school-related stress.

By sharing my experiences and the lessons I've learned along the way, I can help others. I know the desperate feelings of struggle, disappointment, and failure. I hope I can encourage you as you encounter these feelings as well.

School can be tough with all the pressure to make good grades. The educational system penalizes students who don't meet their version of performance criteria. It's sad because we're all on different levels and have different skills and talents. I don't think the grading system is entirely flawed, but I feel we should also be graded on effort because we all have varying potentials in different areas. For example, I have a good friend with dyslexia who works harder than anyone I know, yet unfortunately, her grades don't reflect it.

In eighth-grade art class, my painting wasn't scored based on the performance of others. Instead, my art teacher graded on effort and how we applied what we learned in class. I know if other student's abilities set the benchmark I was measured by, I would've been at the lower percentile because it's safe to say, art isn't my calling.

However, we live in a nation that ranks and classifies us based on our standardized test scores. First, there must be a better way to test our knowledge than using standardized tests. Second, Van Gogh would've crushed everyone on the art section, if there was one, but maybe not scored so well in the other tested areas. Overall, his cumulative score may have been average or even below average because, as we know, art isn't a part of standardized tests. Who's to say this system is an accurate definer of success? And who's to say you're not smart and talented if you don't make straight A's?

I've been the bottom guy before, and I've known the feeling of hopelessness when things don't make sense. Effort and hard work don't seem to impact the situation. If you can relate, I encourage you to keep pressing on to your true potential without allowing outside opinions to bring you down. Don't let their labels, ranking, and classification of you define you. It's important to focus on doing your best and avoid comparison.

> BELIEVING IN YOURSELF AND IN GOD THROUGHOUT TOUGH TIMES IS ESSENTIAL.

My goal is to help you reach *your* maximum potential. I hope you're inspired to set and go after your goals, be a better you, and increase your productivity. Life's circumstances, unfortunately, will slowly try to turn your motivational pep talks from, "I can do this," into "Maybe this is too hard for me." There will be lies whispered in your head, and people who'll say things to try to minimize and destroy your confidence. Believing in yourself and in God throughout tough times is essential.

Imagine you're in a pitch-black cave with only a lantern. This lantern represents hope guiding your way. Through tough times, darkness surrounds you, and to see the path before you, you must keep your lantern ignited with hope. This light is fueled by faith in God and the hope He provides for the future. With faith and hope, you navigate through the darkness until you reach the mouth of the cave, where then you'll see powerful, natural light provided by the radiant sun. This lantern of hope gives you assurance there's an eternal light shining somewhere even if you can't see it until you reach the end of the cave. If you carry this lantern around everywhere you go, you'll have the necessary courage to stay the course despite tough times.

Jeremiah 29:11 (NIV) says, "*For I know the plans I have for you,*" *declares the Lord,* "*plans to prosper you and not to harm you, plans to give you hope and a future.*"

We need to become sold out for God and the purpose He has for us. People might criticize you, call you crazy, or tell you your dreams are absurd. However, when you have this *God-confidence,* you'll be able to act only in fear of God and not react in fear of others.

God's got big plans for your life—keep pressing on! Because *you* are unique, it's important to know one size doesn't fit all. Therefore, I'll provide many solutions to the obstacles we face. Each person needs to find methods that consistently work for them in the long-term.

Every day, we can impact those around us without even trying. In positive or negative ways, humans learn or change by watching others. My hope is for you to take these nugget lessons and become successful in all areas of life. Then, others, seeing the change in you, will be positively impacted as well. It's a ripple effect, and you can be the first drop that potentially influences your whole school, community, and the world.

Did you know the Smoky Mountains forest fire in 2017 started when two teenage-boys were messing around, throwing lit matches on the ground? It was no longer fun and games when one match caught brush on fire. The fire spread rapidly after ninety mph winds picked up a few days later. The firefighters were unable to contain it. One match caused Tennessee's deadliest forest-fire of the century, encompassing 17,000 acres, killing fourteen people, and burning 2,400 buildings.[1]

This tragic example shows how fire can be destructive and widespread. But what if we could positively ignite the flames of authenticity, purpose, and love in those around us? What if this message of hope spread like wildfire? We could potentially shape the culture around us by becoming the change we want to see.

It only takes a spark. Today, let's start building each other up with love and encouragement instead of sowing destruction with seeds of hate and jealousy. This encouragement would be a great habit to focus on first.

It's my prayer for this book to be a catalyst that ignites the fire of the trailblazer within you. May you launch out of the cultural norms, lead and not follow, and land into your God-appointed destiny. These are the years to trailblaze your path. Let's get started.

Reinforcements:

- Setting good habits today sets us up for success tomorrow.

- The 21/90 rule states it takes twenty-one days to create a habit and ninety days to create a lifestyle.

- Be careful to not allow labels, rankings, and classifications define you.

- Focus on doing your best and remember not to compare yourself to others.

- Learn to *act* in fear of God and not *react* in fear of others.

Pause and Ponder:

1. List two habits you would like to develop. Then list two habits you would like to break.

   _____

   _____

   _____

   _____

2. What realistic processes do you think would get you there?

   _____

   _____

   _____

   _____

2

DEFINING SUCCESS

We all have different visions of success and goals we aspire to achieve. You can't fulfill your dreams when you're following the crowd. Therefore, it's vital to trailblaze *your* path. To be a trailblazer is to be the first person to do something new. Despite our similarities, no one in the human race has the same fingerprint. Likewise, your purpose in this world is like no other. A trailblazer forges his path, pioneers his purpose, and discovers his destiny.

What does success mean to you? Is success simply getting a coveted job, establishing a family, and owning a house with a white-picket fence? Or, perhaps success is first-class, private yachts, and Maserati's? Or, does the number of followers you have on social media define success?

Success is a word that means several different things, depending on the individual. According to Merriam-Webster, the definition of success is: obtaining a favorable or desired outcome. Your definition of success could be very different from mine because we desire different things.

Business Insider, the largest business news site on the web, researched some of the world's most influential and impressive people to uncover what they had to say about success. From Maya

Angelou to Winston Churchill, each person gave a completely different definition. Legendary investor Warren Buffet measures success by how well-liked he is. Microsoft cofounder Bill Gates believes it's about making an impact on society. Inventor Thomas Edison worked sixty consecutive hours on occasion and quoted, "Success is 1% inspiration, 99% perspiration."

Stephen Covey, bestselling author of "*The Seven Habits of Highly Effective People*," sums it up well. He says, "If you carefully consider what you want to be said of you in the funeral experience, you will find your definition of success."[1]

For me, success is enjoying life while intentionally impacting people through God's love, which foregoes the typical terms involving money or status. Unfortunately, many people die with regret because they thought wealth and status would leave them content. The only thing we take to heaven is the number of souls we lead to Christ. The car and the house must stay.

I challenge you to consider whether your view of success will truly bring fulfillment. Apostle Paul shared his definition of success in Philippians 3:8:

"I count all things to be loss in view of the surpassing value of knowing Christ Jesus my Lord, for whom I have suffered the loss of all things and count them but rubbish in order that I may gain Christ."

To Paul, everything was trash compared to knowing Jesus. Money, comfort, popularity, grades, trophies, and appearances were worthless and meaningless. But knowing Christ trumped all, and no one or nothing could take that away from him. Paul was a wise man. Maybe we should take note.

ATTITUDE

No matter our definition of success, our attitude is the vehicle that gets us there. You may have heard, "Your attitude determines your altitude." Do you want to drive in a beat-up car that breaks down every 300 miles, or would you rather go farther and faster in a jet plane?

Positive attitudes invite positive results. Negative attitudes invite negative results.

A person with a positive attitude exudes confidence, sincerity, determination, and enjoyment in all they do. They don't let the hurdles of life trip them up. They nurture their skills to overcome obstacles. They avoid naysayers, believing in themselves and what they're capable of. They say:

"I can do all things through Christ who gives me strength" (Philippians 4:13 NLT).

Attitude makes a difference every hour of every day, in everything we do. What we get out of life depends on the attitude we put into it. It's the law of reaping and sowing. You sow joy, and you reap joy. You sow discontentment, and you reap discontentment.

> POSITIVE ATTITUDES INVITE POSITIVE RESULTS. NEGATIVE ATTITUDES INVITE NEGATIVE RESULTS.

It's always a choice, and I've chosen poorly many times. When I have a poor attitude, situations appear worse than they really are, and my productivity goes down drastically. If I have a bad attitude, I work out of dread and not pleasure.

However, when we have a positive attitude, we whistle while we work. We know there's a solution to all problems as long as we keep searching until we figure it out. We know the satisfaction of a job well done. Therefore, we do all things with a spirit of excellence. Not only does this improve the quality of our work, but it also helps make the most out of situations and allows us to have more fun throughout the process.

LIFESTYLES OF THE SUCCESSFUL

We're known by the company we keep. Successful people surround themselves with people who're optimistic and driven with similar aspirations. We need people who'll pick us up when we've fallen and cheer us on as we venture down our road to success. Establishing great relationships allows us to keep each other accountable in achieving our goals. Accountability keeps us going when we want to quit. When we share the journey, the process is much more enjoyable. These people encourage us to reach our fullest potential.

Successful people are continually learning. It's important to be teachable. When we interact with people, we should be good listeners and glean from others' experiences. We should also be avid readers in a wide array of subjects. Take note of what's going on in the world and stay abreast of new and emerging technology. Read God's word daily and heed its wisdom.

Successful people challenge their self-perceived limitations. They aren't satisfied with the status quo. This fight for victory produces growth and welcomes opportunities for advanced methods that will improve outcomes. They look for ways to streamline processes and solve problems.

Successful people wake up early, go to bed early, and make their beds every day. Their health is a priority. They know when to rest and recharge. They watch TV in moderation. They incorporate to-do lists into their calendar, strategically scheduling time to do them. They invest in relationships and adapt to change quickly. They don't give up easily, but instead, they work hard and avoid sitting on the sidelines. They take action because they aren't merely dreamers but doers. After they watch and learn, they implement and enhance.

Which of these things can you start incorporating into your daily routine?

SUCCESS IN YOUR JOB

One of the most significant decisions we will make is our career path. Contrary to popular belief, we shouldn't allow money to drive our decision of occupation. From my observation, doing what you feel called to do is more important than the almighty dollar.

The average person spends a third of their life at work accumulating 90,000 hours over the course of a lifetime.[2] With this statistic in mind, shouldn't it be obvious to find a job that interests and motivates you?

When we're genuinely truly passionate about something, it won't feel like work, and we'll naturally become good at it. *Passion produces excellence, which leads to promotion.* Perhaps more importantly, it won't seem like the dreaded work week, in which we live only for the weekends. Ideally, we'll learn this early on, rather than discovering it the hard way when it seems too late and too inconvenient to restart.

Money is a necessity of life, but why not find a way to make money doing something you love to do? Many argue money makes life easier. Even if it does, it doesn't equate to happiness. I'd rather be broke and happy than rich and miserable.

When you find your dream job, it won't feel like you're wasting your time at work punching your timecard in exchange for a paycheck. A career with a deeper purpose is more fulfilling. Nevertheless, many people I know say their job is a means to an end. It's their way of providing for their family. Yet even then, their job has a purpose.

I feel it's important to interject one note of encouragement here. It's completely okay to have no idea what career you want to pursue in the future. I still have no idea where my career path will take me. However, it's smart for us to start thinking about our interests, passions, and talents. When we discover something that encompasses these three things, that's when we'll truly flourish.

Shakespeare said, "I've seen many unhappy kings, and also many happy shoemakers."[3] The shoemaker found satisfaction in his work and was grateful for every cent he earned. However, enough will never be enough for the king. He has everything he wants but is still unhappy because his heart is always wanting more. He compares his kingdom to others and will never feel completely satisfied.

We need to discover and pursue God's purpose for our lives whether it's a shoemaker or a king. Life shouldn't revolve around our job but around Jesus. Money is okay as long as we don't become greedy. Our career shouldn't define who we are because we're so much more than that. According to a 2018 report from the Bureau of Labor Statistics, the average person changes jobs twelve times during his or her career.[4] If we can find joy no matter where we are or what job we hold, then we will find success.

FINDING A WORK/LIFE BALANCE

Most successful people take breaks to step back, relax, and enjoy their successes. Even God rested on the seventh day and looked back over each of His accomplishments and said, *"It was very good"* (Genesis 1: 31). This should inspire us to step away from our work and see the bigger picture. We shouldn't live to work. We work to live.

Harold Samuel Kushner, a prominent Jewish American rabbi, speaks about the work/life balance. "Nobody on their deathbed has ever said, 'I wish I had spent more time at the office.'"[5]

In the end, nobody wishes they earned more money, drove a faster car, or earned a higher degree. Instead, most wish they'd spent more time establishing healthy relationships.

Achieving success shouldn't make us sacrifice the things that matter the most: God, our relationships, and our health.

Reinforcements:

- A trailblazer forges his path, pioneers his purpose, and discovers his destiny.

- The definition of success is deeply individualized.

- Your attitude is your vehicle to success.

- Decide on a career path based on your purpose and passion rather than money.

- Don't let your road to success be a sacrifice of what matters the most: God, relationships, and your health.

Pause and Ponder:

1. What's your definition of success?

   _____

   _____

   _____

   _____

   _____

2. Lists some of your interests, passions, and talents.

   _____

   _____

   _____

   _____

   _____

3. What are some career paths encompassing these three things?

   _____

   _____

   _____

   _____

   _____

3

TRAINING TO BE DISCIPLINED

Discipline is one of the most fundamental concepts in this book, and you'll find its theme sprinkled throughout many of the chapters. It takes discipline to be consistent, to come back from failure, to manage your time, to find balance, to resist temptation, and to test and practice your faith. In fact, without discipline, we'd blow wherever the wind would carry us.

One thing highly accomplished people have in common is discipline. It's my goal to instill this trait within you. Then, when the wind blows, you won't wind up in the gutter. The disciplined do what they need to do when they need to do it, whether they feel like it or not. When we contemplate important decisions, we may hear differing viewpoints within ourselves. Sometimes, the wrong voice wins the battle, but I'm always glad afterward when I follow the disciplined voice.

Discipline steers our ships. If every wind of doctrine can easily sway our decisions and beliefs, then we're unstable and double-minded.

"Do not waver, for a person with divided loyalty is as unsettled as a wave of the sea that is blown and tossed by the wind... Their loyalty is divided between God and the world, and they are unstable in everything they do" (James 1: 6-8, NLT).

Without discipline, we end up ship-wrecked or lost at sea with no aim or purpose, so we eventually find ourselves either stranded on a deserted island or drowning.

However, discipline steers our ships forward with just enough power to keep us from getting pushed around by the waves. Discipline points the front end of our ship into the waves to plow through them safely. Without this proper aim, our ships would roll over and sink if we got sideswiped by a strong enough wave.[1]

FOLLOWING THE INNER WITNESS

Humans are comprised of body, soul, and spirit. Each has its own voice, and we need to differentiate which one is speaking. Desire and craving are the voices of the body, reason and feeling are the voices of the soul (mind, will, and emotions), and conscience is the voice of the human spirit.

We all know Pinocchio and the famous Jimmy Cricket, who said, "Let your conscience be your guide." Everyone has a conscience, a gut feeling to tell us right from wrong. Its inner witness reveals the heart of man. When we listen, it leads us to make the right decisions, but we can choose to ignore it. Unfortunately, if we ignore our conscience long enough, we'll stop being sensitive to its gentle nudging.

> EVERYONE HAS A CONSCIENCE, A GUT FEELING TO TELL US RIGHT FROM WRONG. ITS INNER WITNESS REVEALS THE HEART OF MAN.

The moment we make Jesus the Lord and Savior of our lives, another spirit—the Holy Spirit—comes to live inside every Christian believer. Conscience is to morals (right and wrong) as the Holy Spirit is to truth (your true identity in Christ). The inner witness of the Holy Spirit takes us to a new level, and as John 16:13 says, guides us into all truth.

"But when He, the Spirit of truth, comes, He will guide you into all the truth; for He will not speak on His own initiative, but whatever He hears, He will speak; and He will disclose to you what is to come."

Giving the Holy Spirit priority in our lives requires extreme self-discipline. We need to read the Bible and wholeheartedly study the scriptures, getting the word deep into our hearts. We also need to speak the word. We are who the Bible says we are, and we can do what the Bible says we can do. Then, we need to be doers of the word. We follow and obey the instruction of the Bible.

In addition to all this, we must instantly obey the voice of the Holy Spirit. We don't do what we want to do or what we feel like doing, but we do what the Holy Spirit tells us to do. By following the Holy Spirit, we will find prosperity and good success!

"Listen carefully, my dear child, to everything that I teach you, and pay attention to all that I have to say. Fill your thoughts with my words until they penetrate deep into your spirit. Then, as you unwrap my words, they will impart true life and radiant health into the very core of your being. So above all, guard the affections of your heart, for they affect all that you are. Pay attention to the welfare of your innermost being, for from there flows the wellspring of life. Avoid dishonest speech and pretentious words. Be free from using perverse words, no matter what! Set your gaze on the path before you. With fixed purpose, looking straight ahead, ignore life's distractions. Watch where you're going! Stick to the path of truth, and the road will be safe and smooth before you. Don't allow yourself to be sidetracked for even a moment or take the detour that leads to darkness" (Proverbs 4:20-27 TPT).

Every time I ignored my inner witness and gave in to peer pressure, I regretted it afterward. It takes discipline to consider the outcome or consequence of an action before doing it. Feeling good at the moment isn't worth the result of giving in to temptation.

STANDING UP TO PEER PRESSURE

Way easier said than done, but we also need to train ourselves to stand firm under peer pressure. Peer pressure is the urge to go with the flow and do what everyone else is doing simply because everyone else is doing it. We've all experienced it. It can be as minor as getting a trendy haircut or as challenging as being confronted with alcohol at a party.

We need a game plan. We need to know how we're going to react if someone pressures us to do something we know is wrong. When we're disciplined to the truth and sensitive to the Holy Spirit, the pressure to do something contrary to our beliefs minimizes, if not disappears. We won't consider any alternative, and our response is like a natural reflex.

As a people-pleaser, I find this is sometimes difficult. Sadly, most people don't have your best interests in mind. So, when we feel pressure from others to go along with the crowd, we should ask ourselves, "Will this action hurt God?" When we're more concerned with pleasing God than pleasing people, it will become easier to do the right thing.

A great college and NFL football star lost his whole career because others fueled his motivation. Eddie Lacy finished three years as a star running back for the best college football program in history, Alabama. The fan base of Alabama was extremely supportive and motivated him to get better each day. He was then drafted high in the second round in the NFL to the Green Bay Packers.

When Hurricane Katrina hit his hometown hard in Louisiana, he and his family lost pretty much everything. Lacy dealt with heartbreak and stress after the incident through the comforts of his family and food. According to Lacy, "It was southern Louisiana cooking, so nothing healthy."

He used the family meals to comfort his loss and in turn, gained quite a bit of weight in the offseason while on a contract for the Packers. He returned the next season with about forty extra pounds and didn't perform how Green Bay had envisioned for him to play. Fans and the media were brutal. He should've ignored their negative comments, but he didn't. He no longer heard the praise he'd heard at Alabama. He succumbed to the fans' negativity into a downward spiral of lost hope and more food.

I felt bad for him because he was such a star athlete, but he became known for *eating his way out of the NFL*. There will always be naysayers, and if you don't know how to ignore them, they'll crush you, as they did Lacy.

The Seattle Seahawks offered him over four-hundred thousand dollars to reach a certain weight over ten months. He failed. That was his last chance, and he left the NFL in 2017.[2]

He sacrificed his health and his football career because of people's opinions of him. Life is more than football and money. I'm so glad he now claims to live happily with his family without football.

The truth is, you'll never be able to make everyone happy. Appeasing everyone is an unreachable goal. You must learn the discipline to act and make decisions for yourself. You might then ask, *wouldn't that be selfish?* If the decision is for your well-being and mental state, real friends and supporters will understand and support you. Standing up the first time will ensure others won't try to take advantage of you a second time.

DISCIPLINE TO DO THE RIGHT THING

Great Britain's attempt to appease Germany during World War II was almost deadly for the whole world. Prime Minister of Great Britain, Neville Chamberlain, tried to bring peace in an official agreement known as Appeasement. The deal with Hitler promised that Germany would no longer take over any more neutral states after Great Britain allowed Germany to control the German-speaking side of Czechoslovakia.

Hitler's cravings, however, weren't satisfied for long, and he knew Great Britain was passive and desperate to avoid a face-off against them. Therefore, he seized more territory until his power seemed to overthrow Britain. Great Britain knew they were in trouble and needed some serious help fast because war was breaking loose.

In 1941, The United States intervened in World War II on behalf of the allied powers, the greatest nations of them being Great Britain, France, and the Soviet Union against the axis powers Germany, Italy, and Japan.[3] Chamberlain should've made a more serious threat from the beginning when Britain was still stronger than Germany and the Nazi army. He should've known Hitler wouldn't have been satisfied until Germany became the superpower of the world. If the United States hadn't intervened on behalf of the allied powers in 1941, who knows whether Germany would've taken over the world.

This is an important lesson for us all. We should have enough discipline to take a stance for what we believe in and then be bold about enforcing it. Discipline establishes healthy and respectful boundaries. For some, you can give them an inch, and they'll take a mile.

A good leader doesn't allow others' opinions of him to dictate his actions. A good leader accepts they can't make everyone happy and only makes decisions based on what's best for the majority. No matter what decisions you make, don't expect everyone to be on board with it.

I was asked to cheat a few times in school. In one instance, I was offered a decent amount of money for a long essay we had to do. Although tempting, each time I declined because I knew it was the right thing to do. I know the punishment for being on the giving end of cheating is equally as bad as the receiving end. Our friendship didn't end, and they've never asked to cheat from me again. They respected my decision, and we still talk like nothing happened.

Initially, your resistance to peer pressure may be a feeble, timid attempt. But the more you discipline yourself, the easier it will become. And take heart when some reject you for resisting their control. Many others will respect this boldness. Remember, if you don't stand for something, you'll fall for anything.

A DISCIPLINED MIND

The idea that disciplined people are always positive go-getters who never take a day off is a big misconception. They still have self-doubt somedays and feel lazy other days like everyone else. The difference is the disciplined don't allow fear, doubt, or fatigue to immobilize them. They're always moving forward toward their goals.

IF YOU'RE WILLING TO DREAM, BUT NOT WORK, YOU MIGHT AS WELL GO BACK TO SLEEP.

Sometimes, we look at someone driven and hardworking and ask, "Where do you get the energy to accomplish so much?" However, if we want to know the secret to their success, what we should be asking is, "How did you become so disciplined?"

Inspiration and motivation will come and go. If you're willing to dream, but not work, you might as well go back to sleep. You'll never see your dream fulfilled without establishing it first in your mind and then following it through with your actions. Keep your eyes on the goal and your mind on the game plan. Any negative thought that gets in the way must be taken captive.

A professor at Durham University cites a researcher in her book who clocks inner speech at an average pace of 4,000 words per minute. That means the speech floating around in your head is ten times faster than verbal speech.[4] Wow! That's either a really good pep-talk or a really bad bashing. We must be incredibly careful about what we think because that's what we'll become. In our minds, we birth the vision for who we want to be, and there we also battle to fulfill that vision. I wonder how many people never reach their full potential because they gave up the fight too easily.

Take exercise, for example. How many of us retreat or ease up at the first pulse of pain? We don't like to feel uncomfortable. And yet, the very thing we try to avoid is what pushes us past our imagined limitations.

Eliud Kipchoge, the best marathoner in history, said, "If you don't rule your mind, your mind will rule you."[5] On hard runs, my mind gives up long before my body does. In my mind, sirens scream at me to stop and slow down. I must tell myself to relax and keep going—I'm almost there.

It's time to get comfortable at feeling uncomfortable. We're capable of so much more than our minds can conceive. Take authority over the voices telling you to quit. You're so much stronger than you know.

SELF-DISCIPLINE WHEN NO ONE IS WATCHING

How do you know you have self-discipline unless it's tested? The more it's tested through the fire, the stronger it'll be.

Our discipline is most tested when we're alone, and no one is watching. It's much harder to make the right decisions when we don't have someone else to keep us accountable. The truth is, God is always watching, and whether people are or aren't around shouldn't influence our actions. But it does.

As you know, I run cross country, and we train six days a week year-round. Every summer, while on vacation, my coaches expect me to continue my training no matter what. Training on my own is much harder when no coach or teammates are observing or pushing me. And when I'm on vacation, there's no accountability. In late July of 2018, I had the hardest time trying to stick with my training. We went to Florida, and it was over ninety degrees every day. Back home, I knew the team was still training hard, but here, I had to go it alone.

All I had was a text message from my coach on what workout they were doing every day at practice. I admit it was intimidating, but I knew I had to do it. Doing mile repeats six times in ninety-five degrees with a warmup and cool down by myself was probably the hardest day that week.

I could've skipped or cut corners because no one would've ever known. However, I did everything the coach texted, even though I wanted to shorten it almost every day. After the vacation, I was proud of myself for following through with my training without accountability. And when I rejoined the team the following week, I never missed a beat.

There's a quote posted on the wall of our school's weight room that reads, "The true test of a man's character is how he conducts himself when no one is watching." This quote was something I thought about when I woke up before everyone else and hit the trail each day. I felt alone, but I was not. God was looking down on me every step of the way.

I don't want to give the wrong impression this vacation or my life is a total working-grind. After I ran in the morning, I chilled by the pool and beach the remainder of the day, listening to the relaxing sound of the crashing waves. To me, that one grueling hour was worth the pain.

My former football coach once said his daughter was frustrated because she felt her playing time in basketball wasn't enough. So, he asked her, "How much time outside of practice are you working on getting better at the game?"

She thought, then shrugged, "Not too much."

He then asked, "Do you think your playing time would be different if you had spent more time on your own to improve your game?"

Self-discipline requires practice, but it will yield a great outcome over time. I look at the successes of other people and sometimes get jealous or feel impatient with my journey. What we don't see is the many failures and the hours of practice it took for others to get there.

To sum it up, God is more interested in our character than He is in our comfort.

What do you do when no one is watching? Are you tempted to take the easy route, cheat, or sweep something under the rug? Keep in mind, what's done in the dark will eventually be brought into the light.

THE HARDSHIP OF BEGINNING

Even for the disciplined, starting something new is often
the hardest part. The hardest
mountain you'll climb is the
one before you get there.

> GOD IS MORE INTERESTED IN
> OUR CHARACTER THAN HE IS
> IN OUR COMFORT.

Excuses sound reasonable to us and make us feel justified for remaining unchanged. Tyrese Gibson said, "Excuses sound best to the person that's making 'em up."[6] The disciplined person acts regardless of circumstances, what others tell them, and what their mind tricks them into believing.

Honestly, the hardest part of my run is right before I get started. I look down at my watch, and I see all zeros—zero time elapsed, zero distance, and zero pace. At this point, I know I'm the farthest from the end. I know it's going to be hard. But still, I begin. After starting, I'm not tempted to quit because momentum carries me mile-by-mile, closer to the finish. I push through the pain because I have an end goal.

Before I know it, I finish. What a feeling that is to conquer my battle, mentally and physically. I never regret it. I look down at my watch and am grateful to see a successfully completed run.

PURPOSEFUL DIRECTION

Stephen Covey, author of *7 Habits of Highly Effective People,* made an intriguing quote saying, "Only the disciplined are truly free. The undisciplined are slaves to moods, appetites, and passions."[7]

So true. Those times when I'm tired or tempted to give in to peer pressure, it's my discipline that pushes me through. I'm more fulfilled because I'm moving in a purposeful direction. Discipline says you want something without even speaking it. It's not lip service. It's integrity, blood, sweat, and tears. You're going places, and your discipline is driving you there.

Reinforcements:

- An undisciplined life is dangerous, unstable, and aimless.

- It takes discipline to consider the outcome or consequence of an action before doing it.

- A good leader doesn't allow others' opinions of him to dictate his actions.

- Discipline is a learned trait that must be tested and strengthened.

- Discipline is more dependable than feelings because it knows what you *need* to do, not what you *want* to do.

- Motivation comes and goes; discipline stays and prevails.

- God is always watching the decisions we make.

- The disciplined person acts regardless of circumstances, what others tell them, and what their mind tricks them into believing.

- Discipline says you want something without even speaking it.

Pause and Ponder:

1. What's your biggest excuse that's holding you back from achieving your goals?

_____

_____

_____

_____

2. What truth is God revealing to you that debunks this excuse?

_____

_____

_____

_____

3. How would your life benefit from living more disciplined?

_____

_____

_____

_____

4

DISCOVERING YOUR IDENTITY

These are the years of self-discovery—learning who we are and what we stand for, finding out our passions and talents, tapping into our dreams, and choosing paths to make them realities.

We're all created by an almighty God, made in His image, and destined for great things. How we view ourselves affects so many things like how we carry ourselves, what risks we're willing to take, and how we come across to others. For example, in a study of teenage girls' self-image, participants who rated themselves as socially unpopular were sixty-nine percent more likely to gain weight than those who considered themselves popular. Other research has found that people with positive self-image are less likely to engage in promiscuous sexual behavior as well.[1]

Often, our view of ourselves is tainted and inaccurate. We can be harshly critical of ourselves, which is detrimental to our potential. Our self-portrait affects how others see us and how we see the world. We need to do some major introspection in this area.

How do you view yourself? Are you a glass half full or a glass half empty type of person? Do you often have feelings that you aren't good enough or that you don't matter? Does fear of rejection or ridicule keep you silent? Do you like yourself?

So many struggle with a mistaken identity. The only way to unmask this false sense of self is to open your eyes to how God sees you. He has sought you out and chosen you. God gave His only Son to die on a cross so He can be with you. And Jesus is coming again to receive you so you can dwell with Him forever. All He asks is that you choose Him back.

"You formed my inward parts; You wove me in my mother's womb. I will give thanks to You, for I am fearfully and wonderfully made; wonderful are Your works, and my soul knows it very well... How precious also are Your thoughts to me, O God! How vast is the sum of them! If I should count them, they would outnumber the sand" (Psalm 139:13-14, 17-18).

It's a Matter of Perspective

Discovering your identity through God is important because this light of truth will uncover the lies the enemy has been feeding you. *"Yet to all who did receive Him, to those who believed in His name, He gave the right to become children of God"* (John 1:12 NIV). Satan hates this and will try anything to keep you from knowing who God created you to be.

You were created for royalty, to reign with King Jesus forever. As a child of God, you're given power through the Holy Spirit to proclaim, *"On earth as it is in heaven"* (Matthew 6:10). You're treasured, valued, and loved more than you'll ever know.

However, the world tells us to find our identity by looking in a one-way mirror. You only see the reflection of who you are right now. When you look at your reflection, you also see what's behind you, your past, and things you aren't proud of. You can get a new haircut or slap some makeup on, but there's no way to really change yourself by looking in this mirror because what you see is what you get.

On the flip side, Christ wants us to have a heavenly perspective—one that clings to hope because it sees a future.

> YOU'RE TREASURED, VALUED, AND LOVED MORE THAN YOU'LL EVER KNOW.

Instead of a mirror, this perspective is like a window. You can see a whole horizon full of potential. You may not be there yet, but because you can see it, you can achieve it. With this perspective, your old ways don't define who you are, and you aren't limited to who you can become. You're not compelled to be content with your present self but will continually develop into the individual God created you to be.

SHARING YOUR GIFTS

Many of us place our identity in what we do, not who we really are. While this is fine and a skill God has given us, our identity is so much more than being a football player or the smart kid in class. It's our character that defines us, not our position, rank, or title.

At the same time, we're all born with unique gifts, talents, strengths, and abilities. As you discover your identity, these things will be revealed to you as well. These are the hidden treasures within you that are there to share with the world around you. We need to dig up and polish these treasures and cultivate them. We aren't meant to be cooped up inside on gadgets throughout the day. We're created for connections and to share the uniqueness God has given us. And for the knuckleheads who don't celebrate you, kick them out of your corner.

We need to be proud of our uniqueness. When we don't use our gifts and unique abilities, it is like having the gift to fly but denying it because others who can't fly may reject us.

Hold your head high, and be you loudly, boldly, and unashamedly. You're so valuable, and the world needs you to take your seat at the table. We're all given a sphere of influence, and your sphere needs to hear your ideas, feel your compassion, see your visions, and experience your unique flavor.

So, come out from your hiding. Now more than ever, people are craving realness. The more vulnerable you are, the more impact you'll have, and the more relatable you'll be to others. At the same time, be aware that your vulnerability may open you up to getting hurt. But as you grow in who you are, the influence of the naysayers will become less and less. Ultimately, if you count the cost and pay the price, you'll reap an incredible return.

LIVING ORIGINAL

I came across a YouTube channel, Vlog Creations, and its tagline reads, "Be alive and really live."[2] It confused me at first, but I kept thinking about it until I discovered the real meaning.

Millions of people are *dead men walking* because they live to the conforms of society and make decisions based on society's norms and expectations. By doing so, they never follow their dreams because they're always following in the footsteps of the people around them. They become puppets controlled by the culture around them.

I don't know about you, but I want to break out of this mold. **I want to punch normal in the face and be fully alive, glorifying Jesus Christ through the authentic person I am.** Are you with me?

God asked Ezekiel, *"Son of man, can these bones live?* (Ezekiel 37). Some of us are so dog tired and discouraged that we live like we're defeated. Many have been beaten down so much they've lost all hope. But like Ezekiel, I'm here to prophesy over these dead bones and speak life into them. I'm here to declare, as you allow God to breathe life into you through the His holy word, the Bible, you'll begin coming alive. As you allow His word to proclaim your identity, you'll experience life in abundance.

My mom always says each one of us reveals a different part of God's nature, and that's why unity in the body of Christ, the church, is glorious. It's why you need me, and I need you because together we see a clearer picture of God. If we aren't living originally, as God made us, a piece of His nature goes missing.

I understand following other's footsteps is a safe route to go. The path is complete, all hinderances removed, and you wouldn't be going it alone. Whereas, if you want to be a trailblazer and live originally, you're often creating your unique path and pioneering your way. There may be obstacles you have to overcome and times you have to stand alone. There's a fork in the road right now. You're standing at the crossroads. Which way do you go?

"Enter by the narrow gate; for the gate is wide, and the way is broad that leads to destruction, and many are those who enter by it. For the gate is small, and the way is narrow that leads to life, and few are those who find it" (Matthew 7:13-14).

Your destiny lies beyond the narrow gate. Your promised land lies over *that* horizon. Let God's word be a lamp unto your feet and a light unto your path. He'll guide you through the uncharted wilderness and equip you to claim new territory for His kingdom.

God has set before you a door that is custom made for you. He's given you the only key that will open that door. If you never walk through that door, that groundbreaking promise land might never be discovered. No one else can fulfill your purpose—only you can.

TURNING BAD INTO GOOD

I recently came across a YouTube video, "Tragedy into Triumph," by Inky Johnson, and found it so inspiring. He shared his story about being games away from signing a contract to enter the NFL, but a terrible injury made this dream shatter like glass. By a miracle, he lived but remained paralyzed in his right arm and hand.

He was angry at this situation for a long time, but then found the good hidden in the rubble of the terrible incident and began to be thankful. He saw how God's plan was more important than the millions of dollars he would've made playing football. Giving money to your family is great, but changing their lives by showing them the love of Jesus is priceless.

He and many of his family were saved, and through his motivational speaking, he's inspired millions of people. So often, our pain becomes our platform. Now, he travels the world, speaking in front of huge crowds all because God redirected this path. By closing one door and opening another, God led Inky Johnson to a more glorious destination than he imagined.[3]

What dream do you feel you would give anything for? Are you willing to hand that dream over to God? Know God may direct you like Inky to an even greater purpose. We must trust God with the good and the bad. Inky had formerly placed his identity in being a successful football player, but now he places his identity in Jesus Christ.

What comes to mind when you think of fire? When I think about the forest fires that blaze far too often out west, I immediately think of destruction, death, and chaos. But there's good that comes from fires. According to research, nutrient levels and soil organic matter both increase drastically after fire. Savannas, covering nearly half the continent of Africa, need many fires in the dry season to recycle nutrients on the surface of the land, allowing rich vegetation to grow again.[4]

So, when you're encountering a bad situation, remember there may be more good than meets the eye. You may think something is bad, but good things can come from it. As a matter of fact, *"God causes all things to work together for good to those who love God, to those who are called according to His purpose"* (Romans 8:28 NIV).

We all have regrets from our pasts. I've definitely had my fair share. No matter what we've done, God never discards us or views us as worthless. He sees us as sheep who've gone astray and became lost—one who He seeks until found. And like the prodigal son, when He sees us approaching Him, He comes running to us. He embraces us instead of scolding us. He trades our filthy rags for a cloak of righteousness. He takes us in and washes us whiter than snow.

When we repent, we're no longer defined by our sin. *"For I will forgive their wickedness and will remember their sins no more"* (Hebrews 8:12 NIV). It's like God presses the redo button and gives us a fresh start. *"Therefore, if anyone is in Christ, the new creation has come: The old has gone, the new is here!"* (2 Corinthians 5:17 NIV).

Your identity is who you are now and who you're becoming. It isn't on who you were or what you've done. No matter your past or current state, it's never too late to redirect yourself to the truth. You'll be received with open arms.

LIVING IN THE IMAGE OF GOD

It's more than merely knowing who you are, but you must also know *whose* you are. You're a son or daughter of the most high king. *"And we all, who with unveiled faces contemplate the Lord's glory, are being transformed into His image with ever-increasing glory, which comes from the Lord, who is the Spirit"* (2 Corinthians 3:18 NIV).

You were made in the image of God and are still being transformed into His image from glory to glory. Most people only go as far as they can see. We like comfort and knowing all the details of the journey. What would happen if we relinquished all control and gave God full reign over our lives? He would take us to new heights where we'd walk in the supernatural and see the impossible.

> YOU WERE MADE IN THE IMAGE OF GOD AND ARE STILL BEING TRANSFORMED INTO HIS IMAGE FROM GLORY TO GLORY.

What do you believe? Will you trust Him completely? With God, the possibilities are endless. Will you live out what you've only dreamed about, and find your true identity in Jesus Christ?

Reinforcements:

- How we view ourselves affects so many things like how we carry ourselves, what risks we're willing to take, and how we come across to others.

- You're treasured, valued, and loved more than you'll ever know.

- When you don't use your gifts and unique abilities, it's like having the gift to fly but denying it because others who can't fly may reject you.

- No one else can fulfill your purpose. Only you can.

- Your identity is who you are and who you're becoming. It's not who you were or what you've done.

Pause and Ponder:

1. Read the following passage about your identity from Ephesians 1:3-11 (TPT). Underline the words or phrases that speak the most to you.

   Every spiritual blessing in the heavenly realm has already been lavished upon us as a love gift from our wonderful heavenly Father, the Father of our Lord Jesus—all because he sees us wrapped into Christ. This is why we celebrate him with all our hearts!

   And he chose us to be his very own, joining us to himself even before he laid the foundation of the universe! Because of his great love, he ordained us, so that we would be seen as holy in his eyes with an unstained innocence.

   For it was always in his perfect plan to adopt us as his delightful children, through our union with Jesus, the Anointed One, so that his tremendous love that cascades over us would glorify his grace—for the same love he has for his Beloved One, Jesus, he has for us. And this unfolding plan brings him great pleasure!

   Since we are now joined to Christ, we have been given the treasures of redemption by his blood—the total cancellation of our sins—all because of the cascading riches of his grace. This superabundant grace is already powerfully working in us, releasing within us all forms of wisdom and practical understanding. And through the revelation of the Anointed One, he unveiled his secret desires to us—the hidden mystery of his long-range plan, which he was delighted to implement from the very beginning of time. And because of God's unfailing purpose, this detailed plan will reign supreme through every period of time until the fulfillment of all the ages finally reaches its climax—when God makes all things new in all of heaven and earth through Jesus Christ.

Through our union with Christ we too have been claimed by God as his own inheritance. Before we were even born, he gave us our destiny; that we would fulfill the plan of God who always accomplishes every purpose and plan in his heart.

2. Why do you think those jumped out to you the most?

_____

_____

_____

_____

5

WINNING THE MIND GAME

Henry Ford once said, "Whether you think you can, or you think you can't, you're right."[1] Our thoughts hold great power. What you think and believe does influence the outcome.

The struggle lies in the battlefield of the mind. In every decision we make, we have conflicting voices in our head warring over our destiny. The voice we listen to influences our course of action. We win our battles when *we are taking every thought captive to the obedience of Christ,* as 2 Corinthians 10:5 instructs. Otherwise, we lose our battles when we allow our feelings to rule our decisions.

Have you ever noticed what thoughts consistently fill your mind? Maybe you're a worrier who replays troublesome scenarios over and over. Or, maybe your thoughts are filled with lists of things to do, and you're always planning. Or, perhaps you're a dreamer, creating big ideas with your vivid imagination. Or, you could be an analytical thinker pondering the probabilities and the what-ifs. More than likely, you're a mix of all of these.

Truth of the matter is, many times we think unconsciously, meaning we aren't aware of what's running through our mind. Michael Halassa, an assistant professor in the department of brain and cognitive sciences at MIT, said that the brain never actually stops *thinking* in a broader sense of the word. Most thoughts are actually happening in the background without us being aware of them, and "there's not really a way to turn these things off."[2] So, how are we supposed to take these thoughts captive?

As soon as we become aware of a thought that is contrary to God's word, we should capture it like a prisoner of war. 2 Corinthians 10:5 also instructs us to "*destroy speculations and every lofty thing raised up against the knowledge of God*" because if we think something long enough, we start to believe it. Then, it begins shaping who we are.

We're encouraged to think about "*Whatever is true, whatever is noble, whatever is right, whatever is pure, whatever is lovely, whatever is of good repute—if there is any excellence and if anything worthy of praise—dwell on these things*" (Philippians 4:8). We need to think about what we're thinking. When we allow our minds to run wild, our thoughts can quickly lead us down a path to destruction.

So, like it or not, you're the next contestant in The Mind Game. Let me share some strategies that will help you win this battle.

BELIEVE YOU CAN

The story goes that as a child, Thomas Edison came home from school one day and gave his mother a paper from the teacher. Thomas said, "My teacher gave this paper to me and told me only to give it to my mother." His mother's eyes were tearful as she read the letter out loud to her child:

"*Your son is a genius. This school is too small for him and doesn't have enough good teachers for training him. Please teach him yourself.*"

One day, he was looking through old family things. Suddenly, he saw a folded paper in the corner of a drawer in a desk. He took it and opened it up. On the paper was written: "*Your son is addled [mentally ill]. We won't let him come to school anymore.*"

Edison cried for hours, and then he wrote in his diary: *"Thomas Alva Edison was an addled child that, by a hero mother, became the genius of the century."*[3]

Because of his mom, he went on to become one of the greatest inventors. His mom believed in him before anyone else did and led him to believe in himself the same way. In a rare interview of Edison in 1907, he spoke of his mother, saying, "She was the most enthusiastic champion a boy ever had, and I determined right then that I would be worthy of her and show her that her confidence was not misplaced."[4]

Do you whole-heartedly believe you can do anything you set your mind to? As Ronnie Lott once said, "If you can believe it, you can achieve it." When you make your mind up, nothing can stop you. And when doubts come, hold fast to some Winnie-the-Pooh motivation: "You're braver than you believe, and stronger than you seem, and smarter than you think."[5]

MENTAL PREPARATION

The day before cross-country races, our team holds a time of silence so we can visualize our race. As we sit in the stillness with our eyes closed, we let the race play-out in our head like a film. We imagine the good parts of the race, along with the pain we know we will have to push through. We form a mental picture of a run up a steep hill, sweat dripping from our forehead. We see ourselves crossing the finish line, and we salivate for the taste the victory, knowing it's within our grasp.

Visualization is a powerful tool that connects the mind and the body. It helps minimize anxiety and builds confidence, so when we step up to the line, we know we prepared both mentally and physically. We see the goal, and we know what we need to do to get there.

One thing many Navy SEALs learn during Hell Week (when performed successfully) is that the body is ten times stronger than the mind says it is. Throughout these rigorous five days and five nights of four hours maximum of sleep, they say there are points where they must disengage the mind and keep moving, even though they're exhausted. "You learn how to find fuel in the tank, when you thought it was empty."[6]

Our mind will give up much sooner than our bodies will. Sometimes, instead of listening to our thoughts, we need to talk to them. Have a go-to scripture or a motivational quote memorized for when things get tough. Write them on note cards and place them on your bathroom mirror or in your car. Speak these declarations over yourself daily.

MENTAL CAPACITY

Have you ever felt like your brain is going to explode? Or, that it's so full, you couldn't possibly squeeze in any more information? Although the human brain functions a lot like a super high-tech computer, I don't think you'll ever have to worry about running out of storage space.

Paul Reber, professor of psychology at Northwestern University, informs us that the storage capacity for a brain's memory is around 2.5 petabytes (or a million gigabytes). For comparison, if your brain worked like a digital video recorder in a television, 2.5 petabytes would be enough to hold three million hours of TV shows. You would have to leave the TV running continuously for more than 300 years to use up all that storage.[7] Incredible, right?

Despite this information, it's easy for us to feel overwhelmed. Again, the emotions are what get in the way. A good tactic to try in this case is segmenting your tasks by breaking them up into bite-size pieces. For example, if I have a huge book to read for class, rather than waiting until the night before it's due, I'll set aside twenty minutes a night to read. As a side note, I prefer time goals over the number of pages. It's more important for me to understand the book than to rush to get it done. But do what works for you.

WHEN TRYING TO DO A TASK THAT SEEMS OVERWHELMING, FOCUS ON ONE THING AT A TIME.

Some days when I'm not feeling well, I segment my

runs. I tell myself to start the ten-minute warm-up and then see how I feel. Ninety percent of the time, I no longer feel tired after the warm-up, so I go on to continue the full workout. Occasionally, I also incorporate a strides workout into my routine, which is when I sprint the length of three mailboxes, rest for thirty seconds, and repeat. This is a great method of tackling my speed work since I can't sprint very well for a full six miles.

When trying to do a task that seems overwhelming, focus on one thing at a time. Write down a plan of action, prioritize your list, and once you've completed a task, cross it off. Monitoring your progress is very rewarding, and before you know it, you've completed the task.

GET IN THE ZONE

Our mind greatly affects our performance in everything we do. As a result, professional athletes concentrate on building mental focus and mental strength as much as physical conditioning. After a good game, many athletes attribute their success to being in the zone.

It's well accepted by psychologists today that the zone, or *flow*, as some call it, is a real state of being. They define it as a mind-set where people lock-in and become absorbed by what they're doing (i.e., playing their sport). In these instances, we often lose awareness of outside distractions, including time. Our focus is solely on the task before us. Similarly, when in the flow, we're motivated to succeed and often challenged by the job (meaning the task is not perceived as impossible, nor so easy to do that it is worthless to bother doing).[8]

Have you ever been so absorbed in your work that you've lost all track of time? If so, I bet your production level was off the charts. It's easier to get in the zone when you're passionate about something, highly motivated, confident, and challenged. Start noticing what gets you in the zone. These things may be a good indicator of your gifts and calling.

You're Closer Than You Think

Our mind likes to play tricks on us. It will tell us our goal is impossible. *Wait for a better time to attempt that. I don't have what it takes. I'm too busy. I need a break.*

Often, when we feel like giving up, victory is around the corner. I've seen people drop from exhaustion five feet before the finish line. When the crowd cheers for them to keep going, they give their last effort to either get back up or crawl to finish the race.

But what happens when you're exhausted, ready to quit, and you can't see the finish line? There's no crowd to cheer you on. You've no idea how much further until you reach your goal. What then? Do you throw in the towel?

It's interesting that we experience the most opposition right before the victory. The stinking devil knows we're so close. He wants to derail us and keep us from entering into our destiny. He wants us to declare failure five feet from our finish line.

We can't give in to his trickery. To quit now is to sacrifice the whole struggle. You have to *make up your mind to keep pressing on*. Even if you have to crawl, simply move. When the going gets tough, the tough get going. God will renew your strength. Let Him be your source and kick fear, doubt, and fatigue to the curb.

As a team-bonding experience, our cross-country team used to run a hiking trail called Red River Gorge. I went on this trip twice, and one time was a bit more interesting than the other. We set off on a supposedly seven-mile loop (it was longer), but we all got separated after about forty minutes of running.

The trail wasn't marked well, so my friend Austin and I felt like we may have taken some wrong turns because no one was in sight. We yelled repeatedly, but all we could hear was our footsteps, the rustling of the trees, and the whistling sound of the wind. We kept on running for another twenty minutes, hoping we were going in the right direction. We thought for sure we'd taken a wrong turn somewhere. To make matters worse, I was extremely dehydrated. It was a hot July day in the peak of

Kentucky's humidity, and we'd been running for over an hour at that point.

In desperation, I saw a creek, and my survival instincts kicked in. Thinking of nothing but my thirst, I gulped down the creek water. We continued the trail and minutes later, ran into other people hiking in the opposite direction. We asked them for directions, and it turned out we didn't make a wrong turn. We were only one mile from the end. Relieved, we jogged another seven or eight minutes to the end and chugged two water bottles as soon as we got there.

Shortly afterwards, while riding up the road to a restaurant for lunch, I started feeling a little queasy. It didn't take long for me to link it back to the creek water I drank. We finally arrived at the small country restaurant, and I was miserable. I rushed back to the single bathroom, but the door was locked. With no time left and nothing else to do, I puked pure water all over the restaurant floor. It was not my best moment.

The point is, sometimes we believe we're nowhere close to the finish. We think we must have somehow ventured off the path and gotten ourselves lost. When in reality, we've almost made it. Our mind second-guesses our decisions and convinces us we can't go on like this. Because I believed those lies, I drank water from a creek, knowing there's a risk of contamination. And I paid for it later.

God has our back. We must trust Him through the process. Hold tight to the encouragement found in Isaiah 41:10 (TPT). *"Do not yield to fear, for I am always near. Never turn your gaze from me, for I am your faithful God. I will infuse you with my strength and help you in every situation. I will hold you firmly with my victorious right hand."*

DEVELOP A POSITIVE MINDSET

Proverbs 23:7 (TPT) says, *"As he thinks within himself, so he is."* I don't think we realize the power of our thoughts. Before a test, I've heard so many people in school say, "I'm *so* going to fail." Sometimes, people say this because they're trying to sound humble, but you can be confident without having an ego. And belittling yourself isn't exactly humility.

Or, maybe they say this because they didn't fully prepare for the test. In either instance, it's not a healthy thing to say. Go in and take that test with confidence, and you may surprise yourself. If you believe you'll fail, you already have before you even started.

Did you know confidence is directly related to performance? Past research shows when students place higher esteem on their intellectual abilities, the better they perform on academic assignments like tests. Besides cognitive factors such as IQ, confidence is the next best predictor of academic performance, according to a 2012 study published in Learning and Individual Differences.[9]

This is also supported by Dr. Carol Dweks's theory, Growth Mindset. Recent advances in neuroscience have shown us that the brain is far more malleable than we ever knew. When students believe they can get smarter, they understand effort makes them smarter. Therefore, they put in extra time and effort, and that leads to higher achievement.[10]

So how can we improve our confidence? First, we must get rid of all self-limiting beliefs. If you're a Christian and really struggle in this area, know that the Creator of the universe, the One who knows all things, lives inside you. Declare to yourself that you "*have the mind of Christ*" (1 Corinthians 2:16).

Also, surround yourself with a strong support system. Study more, practice more, and ask more questions. Learn to be less defensive and more open to constructive criticism. Communicate without fear of saying the wrong thing. Give yourself the freedom to make mistakes and learn from them.

No one is stupid, and never believe you are. We're going to have weaknesses. Learn how to strengthen them, but don't fret over it. Albert Einstein is linked to a great quote that says, "Everyone is a genius. But if you judge a fish by its ability to climb a tree, it will live its whole life believing that it's stupid."[11] Hone in on your genius ability and cultivate that.

IMPORTANCE OF REFLECTION

No matter what, we should always do our best. Afterward, we should set aside some time to reflect on how we can improve next time. Improvement is so important. We often only reflect after a loss, but I recommend always reflecting—win or lose, success or failure. This one simple mental exercise is the key that separates the elite from the pack.

Maybe next time you can prepare better. Perhaps you got too caught up in the details that you missed the big picture. Maybe you should take better notes. In school, it usually takes me a couple of tests or quizzes to learn what the teacher's expectations are. Every teacher places value on different skills, which means sometimes, we need to adapt to their style to be successful in their class.

Reflection can likewise offer positive reinforcement of what we did right so we can do it again. Personal growth is a daily process, and we may not notice its effects until we've made significant progress. The process could take months or even years, but it will pay off.

Reinforcements:

- What you think and believe influences the outcome.

- "You're braver than you believe, and stronger than you seem, and smarter than you think." – Winnie-the-Pooh quote

- Our mind will give up much sooner than our bodies will.

- A good tactic to try when you're feeling overwhelmed is breaking up your tasks into bite-size pieces.

- Your biggest struggle often comes right before your greatest victory.

- Win or lose, success or failure; time spent reflecting is the key that separates the elite from the pack.

Pause and Ponder:

1. Do you have any overwhelming tasks you're facing that could benefit from segmenting? If yes, outline a quick action plan breaking it down into smaller tasks and include an estimated timeline for completion of each step.

_____

_____

_____

_____

2. What mindset, or self-limiting belief, is holding you back from leaving the pack and launching out of the norms?

_____

_____

_____

_____

6

TAKING A LEAP OF FAITH

In today's world, it's easy to get discouraged and feel a lack of purpose, direction, or significance. Faith in the Lord is crucial for teenagers. More than ever, there's such confusion in our world. Do our lives have meaning, or are we merely a bundle of cells moving together by sheer coincidence?

As a kid, I remember feeling unsurmountable joy, no matter what happened. I lived each day like it was a new adventure. Sadly, this child-like faith has slowly begun to fade as I've grown older. I'm no longer as excited about the little things. I no longer sing at the top of my lungs because I feel like it. And I no longer think of the world so simply as I once did.

The truth of the matter is, life is complicated. But are we over complicating it? When my brother had a sports physical done recently, the pediatrician had to complete his school form. A simple two-option question regarding gender turned into a six-option question. The question is no longer are you male or female, but instead, what sex were you assigned at birth (male, female, or intersex), and how do you now identify your gender (male, female, or other)?

It's no longer wrong or right or night or day. We've literally created fifty shades of gray for everything. There are so many variables. We have more pressures on our identity than ever before. Take social media, for example, we have influencers tell us how to look, what products to buy, the cool lingo to use, how to believe, and the list goes on and on.

The days of going into a store and picking up a product and simply buying it are gone. Now we go online, look at consumer reviews, browse other alternatives, compare prices, and become so overwhelmed it takes an hour to figure out what to buy. Don't get me wrong because I appreciate having options when I'm looking to purchase something. But it can be ridiculously overwhelming at times.

> OUR FAITH IS THE CORNERSTONE OF OUR LIFE.

It's the same with our faith. God always gives us a choice. Otherwise, we'd be nothing more than robots. There's so much deception in the world and so many different variables we've created. We must be on alert and extremely careful about the decision of faith we make.

Some may say there are many pathways to God, or there's no hell, or you're your own God, or there's no God. How we act reflects how we believe. Our faith is the cornerstone of our life. We must ensure that our faith is secure and unwavering because it will influence every aspect of everything we do.

How do we restore the child-like faith that we once had? Who can we fully trust and rely on? Where do we turn when we need help?

WALKING BY FAITH

I believe in the one true God who made the heavens and earth and breathed life into all mankind. His Son, Jesus Christ, was born of the virgin Mary. He died on a cross for my sins, He was resurrected on the third day, and He's coming again for His church. The Holy Spirit is given to every believer as our helper and comforter and one who guides us into all truth. *"Jesus Christ is the way, and the truth, and the life,"* and the only way to God, the Father (John 14:6).

Hebrews 11:1 (NKJV) says, *"Now faith is the substance of things hoped for, the evidence of things not seen."*

No scientist can prove 100% that God is real or not. However, we have evidence all around us that God is with us and providing for us. The beautiful oceans, the sweeping plains, unique animals, and changing seasons are too perfect to be a coincidence.

You can't see the wind, but you see the effects of the wind every day. Does that make wind not real if you can't see it? Both faith and belief come from the same Greek root word, *pistis*. When you believe something, you don't need to see it to know it's there. The same concept applies to believe in a powerful God. 2 Corinthians 5:7 says, *"For we walk by faith, not by sight."* The true test of our faith is believing in things that we cannot see.[1]

However, faith opens our spiritual senses. We begin seeing God move through our circumstances, opening doors for us, and protecting us. We feel His unexplainable peace and his uncontainable joy. We have a knowing deep in our spirit all things will work together for our good. We aren't moved by what we feel, but we're moved by what we believe. Circumstances and opinions don't shake us when we're rooted in our faith.

Without God, there's no anchor to hold on to, no guidance to follow, and little purpose to pursue. Rather than being tossed to and fro and following the loudest voice, we need to hold tight to something bigger than ourselves. When God is our source, our faith in Him gives us a greater purpose, with greater insight, and greater power to cling to.

Faith is the substance of all hope, and without hope, there's no meaning.

TRUSTING GOD'S DIRECTION

When we're faithful, we trust in God's perfect timing and the calling He has for us. Proverbs 3:5-6 says, *"Trust in the Lord with all your heart. And do not lean on your own understanding. In all your ways acknowledge Him, And He will make your paths straight."*

We should invest in God by giving our everything to Him, releasing the things of this world. Investing in God is like investing in a stock that's guaranteed to be successful. We will reap a great return.

Proverbs 2:1-5 (ESV) says, *"My son, if you receive my words and treasure up my commandments with you, making your ear attentive to wisdom and inclining your heart to understanding; yes, if you call out for insight and raise your voice for understanding, if you seek it like silver and search for it as for hidden treasures, then you will understand the fear of the Lord and find the knowledge of God."*

Sometimes, what we think is best for us isn't necessarily what God thinks is best. Thankfully, through His gentle nudges to steer me back on course, He's protected me every time I've strayed. It's our choice whether we listen and obey. The more we resist the voice of the Holy Spirit directing us, the quieter it will become until eventually, we won't hear Him at all.

Do you remember the people of Whoville living on a speck in Dr. Seuss' *Horton Hears a Who?*[2] Only the mighty elephant could make out the faint noise from the village even when they were as loud as they could be. They were desperately trying to be saved from the animal non-believers who wanted to destroy them.

Interestingly, in the real world, an elephant's ears span six feet long and four feet wide. In addition, elephants can communicate through a low rumble up to six miles away through the vibration in its feet. In short, an elephant has one of the best hearing abilities out of all the animals.[3]

Even the most exceptional listeners can become deaf to God when we go astray. When muted to God, who'll we listen to—the evil ways of this world, the cultural norms, the internet, or our pleasure?

Like the doubtful kangaroo, monkeys, and bird in the story, these things will attempt to drown out God's voice. It's so important for us to stay close to Him, to give Him our attentive ear, and to treasure that still, small voice.

God always has open arms when we return even after messing up or being disobedient. He'll come running to you no matter how far you've wandered. Trust the Lord and pull out the biblical compass to help you venture back on the right path.

TRUSTING GOD'S WAYS

One of the most amazing things I've discovered in my life was right behind one of my biggest disappointments. For most of my early life, I had a passion for basketball, and I wasn't too bad. Despite being tall and practicing almost every day at my local YMCA, I tried out for the middle school team in my sixth-grade year and didn't make it. Frustrated, yet optimistic, I worked even harder. Tryouts once again rolled around, and I was confident I'd make it this time. With nervous anticipation, I opened the letter, and my heart sank.

"Unfortunately, you have not been selected to be on this year's team."

I was crushed. The next year, my friend encouraged me to join the cross-country team, and so I did in my eighth-grade year. I found out not making the basketball team both years was a blessing in disguise because I found something better. If I had made the basketball team, I wouldn't have joined the cross-country and track team or discovered my love for running.

I'm much better at running than playing basketball, and I haven't missed it since. I know it was God working it out for me not to make the basketball team, so I'd discover something greater. He loves to trade our good for His best.

I encourage you, don't always look at something face-value then get discouraged when it doesn't go your way. It takes faith to believe there's more than what the human eye can see in the now. Trust that God is working all things out for your best.

The summer before my junior year, many people in my grade were getting jobs. I decided I wanted something to do over the summer to gain work experience and a little bit of extra cash to spend. I decided Chick-Fil-A was the best fit for me, and I had friends working there also. I prayed for a couple of minutes but applying for this job was a decision made of my own will, not God's. I had faith in my choice, and I assumed since it's a Christian-based company, it must be from God, right?

I was excited to work there because I've always loved their food and atmosphere. My mind was set on wanting the job, so I turned in my application. Two weeks passed, and I was confused why they hadn't called me yet. I went to Chick-fil-A, and, as it turned out, they'd lost my application. I was slightly frustrated because I hate to waste time. Nevertheless, I turned in another application.

As you probably know, Chick-fil-A is known for its excellent customer service. Because of this, the hiring process includes three separate interviews. I proceeded through the first two interviews fairly quickly. However, due to vacations and scheduling, I couldn't get my third interview in for a couple of weeks.

After my second interview, I went to a writer's conference with my mom. Before this conference, I had casually tossed around the idea of writing a book but didn't know how to get started or even if I could finish if I did get started. But something inspired me to give it a shot. It was definitely God giving me the nudge.

> WHEN WE FEEL LIKE WE'VE MISSED AN OPPORTUNITY, WE NEED TO HAVE FAITH THERE'S AN EVEN BETTER OPPORTUNITY AWAITING.

I called Chick-fil-A and respectfully declined the third interview, informing them God had something else He wanted me to pursue. God used these delays to prevent me from getting the job. If the process had been at least two days faster, you probably wouldn't be reading this book.

God sometimes has us go through things for a specific purpose. When we feel like we've missed an opportunity, we need to have faith there's an even better opportunity awaiting.

Proverbs 16:9 (NIV) says, *"In their hearts humans plan their course, but the Lord establishes their steps."* We can dream all we want, but God's purpose prevails when we give Him our lives.

SUFFERING TESTS OUR FAITH

Every person will experience suffering. These are times when it's hard to see good in a bad situation. It can be hard to remain faithful in your relationship with God if you feel He should fix your hardships at the snap of your finger.

It takes faith to keep praying when we don't hear a response. When we pray, our trust and commitment are tested. Jeff Pratt, founder of Axiom Global Monastic Community and author of *The Homeward Call*, said, "When we pray, we are trusting God. When He doesn't answer, He is trusting us to keep trusting Him and not lose hope."

We should never be disappointed in God. He's there even when we don't think He is, and He isn't responsible for the destruction. Only good things come from God. The devil wants us to believe God doesn't care about us because He didn't intervene.

Instead, we need to continue to have faith even when things don't look promising. It's our choice. We can blame God, make Him our enemy, and question His existence. Or we can allow this hardship to strengthen the bond we share with God. We can choose to rely on Him through the suffering because He'll sustain us.

FAITH IN MAN

Faith is important, but what we put our faith in is crucial. We should never give a person the place in our heart reserved only for God. People will disappoint us time and again. Why? Because no one is perfect.

We may begin dating in the teenage years. We must be very careful to not esteem anyone higher than we regard God. When this happens, we will always be wanting more and left disappointed. Only God can bring us true fulfillment.

When we put God first, then we can love others and receive their love as we should. God is love, and when we give the author of love His rightful place, everything we do, say, and believe will be through that love. We won't be looking for love, approval, and acceptance in all the wrong places. When we get what we need from God, the Father, then we aren't tempted to look for this from a person, and we're able to give without fear, hesitation, or intimidation.

If a breakup has caused you to dive into a deep depression, it may be wise to ask if your trust and hope is misplaced. While it's much easier said than done, we shouldn't hold on to anything or anyone here too tightly. By this, I mean we should never cling to a person more than we cling to God. He's our hope, and through Him, we can count it all joy.

The things of this world are temporary. People and things of this world come and go. God does not. He'll never leave you or forsake you.

FAITH UNSHAKABLE

I might be a little biased because he's my namesake, but Noah is my favorite person in the Bible. Noah's insurmountable faith boldly withstood the scrutiny that came when people ridiculed him for building an ark without any forecasted rain. Regardless of what others said, he continued to build the ark in obedience to God. His faith was so strong. He even tried to save them, encouraging his naysayers to join him before the flood came. Their rejection didn't discourage or sway him. He kept the faith and stood firm in his belief.

We need to be more like Noah, living a life lined up with our beliefs and not get discouraged upon others' rejection. Noah's strong faith allowed him to listen to God over what others were saying. His bold faith was the reason God chose him.

So, what do we do to have a strong faith that can stand firm in opposition?

We need to get grounded in scripture. We need to abide in God because He shapes our destiny. We need to be content because He fully satisfies. We need to be faithful because He's faithful. We need to surround ourselves with those who'll build us up in faith. And we need to give all the glory to God!

CASTING OUT FEAR

So, if we're not walking in unshakable faith, then what are we walking in? Surprisingly, doubt isn't the opposite of faith. Fear is the opposite of faith, which is a terrible thing to live by.

Fear begins as a 5 o'clock shadow looming with us everywhere we go. It will continue to grow until it brings us into total darkness. It's important to stop it before it gets to that point, so I thought I'd shed some light on the topic.

The Hunger Games was a 2008 American dystopian novel adapted into a film in 2012. The hunger games were established to instill fear into the twelve districts as punishment for a previous failed rebellion.[4] President Snow was not happy when he discovered the Gamemakers gave the heroine, Katniss Everdeen, the highest score of all the tributes. She'd made a shocking display of archery skills when she nailed the apple in a roasted pig's mouth, nearly avoiding the Gamemakers. Later, Snow was infuriated when she placed flowers around her dead ally, Rue, as an act of defiance towards the Capital.

He urged the Head Gamemaker to contain it. He said, "Hope, it is the only thing stronger than fear. A little hope is effective, a lot of hope is dangerous."[5] Snow knew the power he held was only due to the fear he instilled in the districts, and this underdog was giving the districts something to believe in. I'm not going to spoil the movie, but let's say freedom comes when hope overrides fear.

Did you know there are 365 verses in the Bible that instruct us to not fear?[6] That's one for every day of the year. This is an important concept to God. He doesn't want us to live in fear. In fact, the word says, *"For God has not given us a spirit of fear, but of power and of love and of a sound mind"* (2 Timothy 1:7 NKJV).

Don't let fear hold you back from taking that leap of faith. Release the fear and hold onto faith. Your countdown for launch is starting. 10…9…8…7… Get ready! Greatness is up ahead!

Reinforcements:

- When God is our source, our faith in Him gives us a greater purpose, with greater insight, and greater power to cling to.

- Faith is the substance of hope.

- What we think is best isn't always what God thinks is best.

- We should never give a person the place in our heart reserved only for God.

- The opposite of faith is fear. The only thing stronger than fear is hope.

Pause and Ponder:

1. Worry, anxiety, and fear are all signs we aren't trusting God. In what areas is God asking you to trust Him more?

   _____

   _____

   _____

   _____

2. Recall an instance where God protected you by not giving you want you wanted. What good came out of that situation?

   _____

   _____

_____

_____

3. Ask God what He's launching you into. Where is He calling you to be more disciplined? What steps can you take to be more attentive to His call? Take at least five minutes today and seek God's direction here. Write what He lays on your heart during this time.

_____

_____

_____

_____

PART 2:

LEAD

This is Your Captain Speaking:
We Are Gaining Altitude

Let's keep pressing forward into the potential God has for us. This forward progress will be established through the disciplines included in this next section, allowing us to keep our eyes on the goal and lead a life ahead of the pack.

The wolf on the hill is never as hungry as the wolf climbing the hill.[1]

7

SETTING PRIORITIES

I touched on this briefly, but setting priorities is crucial and goes way beyond making to-do lists. It's not about doing the fun and exciting things first, but rather the important things. Prioritizing makes us do things we don't necessarily want to do but need to do.

Within reason, we must embrace work before play, but that's a fine line, however. It's important to find balance here because there will always be work to do, and there will always be something more fun pulling us in the other direction. Sometimes, work will take priority, but other times play will take precedence.

The key here is learning to establish the most important thing at the moment.

ONE AT A TIME

Setting priorities is a vital contributor to maintaining productivity. When you set priorities, you can focus on doing one activity at a time. Multi-tasking, although sometimes necessary, produces less efficiency.

The evidence clearly shows we can't multi-task well. For example, someone is twenty-three times more likely to crash when texting and driving than when driving without distractions.[1]

The reason we can't multi-task isn't entirely our fault. A 2005 study published in the medical journal, *Child Development,* found that teens have "cognitive limitations" because the part of our brain responsible for multi-tasking hasn't fully developed yet.[2]

Keep this in mind the next time you're doing your homework. I challenge you to focus on only the task-at-hand. Cut out all distractions and put away the electronics. Don't think about what you and your friends are planning to do Saturday night. I'm sure you'll be surprised at how much faster and more productive you are when you're focused.

NEEDS VS. WANTS

While establishing priorities, it's wise to learn the difference between a need and a want. For instance, your friends invited you to join them at the mall after school today, but your chemistry teacher decided to announce an unexpected test tomorrow. There are still some concepts you don't understand, and you know you'll be hitting the books hard later. Can you balance both without causing undue stress, or does one take precedence over the other? In this case, it's best to catch your friends another day because you *need* to study.

On the flip side, what if you've been working for a couple of weeks on a big project in U.S. Government class? It's due next week, and your brain is fried. In this situation, you *need* a night off, so a movie night with your friends takes priority.

Many of us in the first situation would be overly optimistic, thinking we could swing both the mall and studying. The more you delay doing something you need to do but don't want to do, the more you'll dread doing it. The more you dread it, the more you'll put it off. Then, as your dread continues to grow, the task keeps getting bigger and bigger. You've created a mountain out of a molehill.

Whereas, if we have a Nike attitude of "Just do it," we put mind over matter. We don't allow our emotions to decide for us. We take control of the situation and tackle it head-on because it's the number one priority right now.

> THE MORE YOU DELAY DOING SOMETHING YOU NEED TO DO BUT DON'T WANT TO DO, THE MORE YOU'LL DREAD DOING IT.

Once you've completed the homework and projects first, the fun stuff will be more enjoyable. Why? Because you've eliminated the dread.

MINDSET

Some of the most accomplished people prioritize their lives by starting each day with the right mindset. Navy SEALs believe a task as simple as making their bed is crucial to being successful all day. Dwayne "The Rock" Johnson wakes up at four o'clock in the morning to workout, which fuels him for the remainder of the day.

Doing something productive and meaningful first thing in the morning puts us in the right frame of mind. Maybe it's prayer and a quick devotional. Maybe it's a morning jog, or perhaps it's looking in the mirror and giving yourself a good pep talk.

During the summer, running first thing in the morning feels great. It starts my day off right, and I'm ready to take on whatever heads my way. If the rest of my day is overwhelming, I can reflect on that one productive feat I've already accomplished.

Sure, I want to hit the snooze button, but I don't. Again, mind over matter. Don't think. Just do. Ironically, most of my best runs are the days I drag myself out the door. The hardest part is getting started.

There are three ways we can do things—the easy way, the hard way, or the right way. Conquer the voice inside your head, saying, "You're too tired; you deserve to sleep in." That's the easy way. Or, "Don't worry about it now. You can get your run in later." That's the hard way because it's challenging to work in a run during an already busy day.

As a cross-country runner, running is a priority. I know when I train best. So, for me, it's best to train in the morning, to get up and run.

Big or small, we need to discover methods to help us remain disciplined, focused, and motivated. A productive morning sets the pace for a productive day.

HEALTHY MIND, HEALTHY LIFE

It's also important to make our health a priority. We only get one earth suit, so we must take care of it. Having good health allows us to live longer and live a higher quality of life. Anyone who has good health should be thankful for it and not take it for granted.

When initially making health a priority, it's tempting to fall into extremes regarding diet and exercise. You'll find I use the word *balance* a lot, and it applies here as well. Small changes done consistently will lead to big results. A big stumbling block on our road to fitness is initiating drastic changes that aren't sustainable.

The payoff for a healthy lifestyle pays dividends for years to come.

WHAT'S AT THE TOP OF YOUR PRIORITY LIST?

It's time to ask yourself—what tops your priority list? Your priorities are usually depicted by how you spend your time and money. Therein lies the things capturing your heart.

Is it the pursuit of money or climbing the ladder of success? Are you consumed with your appearance or the image you project? Why do you do the things you do?

YOU WON'T SEE A U-HAUL BEHIND A HEARSE CARRYING THE DEAD MAN'S VALUABLES TO THE AFTERLIFE.

The thing of it is, you won't see a U-Haul behind a hearse carrying the dead man's valuables to the afterlife.... Sure, these things have their place, but God being first should always and ever be on that trump-card.

When we build our lives around God, many of our problems vanish or seem inconsequential because of the trust we have in Him and His great purposes for us. I desire a mindset that says: Let all I do be done as worship unto God. Hard work apart from God is simply ambition. However, when I submit my work unto God, it becomes worship. He's the reason I do.

Matthew 6:33 says, *"But seek first His kingdom and His righteousness, and all these things shall be added to you."* When we put Him first, He makes sure everything else falls into place.

Abraham Lincoln gave an address to the nation in 1863 about American priorities and how we tend to focus on worldly things such as wealth and power instead of God. He said, *"We have grown in numbers, wealth, and power as no other nation has grown. But we have forgotten God. We have forgotten the gracious hand which has preserved us in peace, and multiplied and enriched and strengthened us...intoxicated with unbroken success, we have become too self-sufficient to feel the necessity of redeeming and preserving grace, too proud to pray to the God that made us!"*

Sadly, our culture continues to lose sight of God, and it's become much worse after this address was delivered over 156 years ago. We need to restore the priority of God. We need to confess our sins and pray for mercy and forgiveness. Then, God will hear and heal our land.

PLACING WORK OVER RELATIONSHIPS

As I mentioned earlier, no one is loading a U-Haul to take with them through the pearly gates. But there are some things we will take with us, and those are souls. The people you lead to Jesus, even those seeds you planted, will join you in heaven. This is why relationships are so vital.

I'm a driven person, and I'm also an introvert. Sometimes, this isn't a great combination for developing quality relationships. Having a driven nature is good, but those with a driven nature tend to drive themselves away from others. Introverts often do the same, so I intentionally make myself get out of my comfort zone.

I set aside time to spend with family and friends. They're more important than my to-do lists and piles of homework accumulating. Relationships bring joy and fulfillment that successful, ordinary work can never deliver.

Work will always be there, yet the relationships we push away may not. What message are we sending when we say we don't have time for someone? Value your work, but value others more. Building relationships are much more important than building our empires.

SETTING PRIORITIES HELPS DECISION-MAKING

Tough decision-making can be stressful. We naturally totter back and forth while making decisions, and often, like hypnosis, we fall under decision-fatigue.

A decision as easy as choosing where to eat can be a struggle, especially with a group that has conflicting preferences. There are many factors to consider, and it overwhelms us. The truth is, you can't go wrong with any place—there will be food on the table, and your hunger will be satisfied.

But what about tough decisions where you're weighing two good things? Roy Disney said, "It's not hard to make decisions when you know what your values are."[3] For me, at least, the best way to evaluate that is by creating a pro/con list for each choice. After doing this, I can make an informed decision based on where my priorities lie. This removes a lot of stress and allows me to become confident in my ultimate decision.

Remember, God, your family, your relationships, and your well-being are on that trump-card. If one of the things you're weighing goes against any of these main priorities, you should consider letting it go. It's also important to pray about any significant decision. We don't want to settle for good. We want God's best for us.

My mom quit her job as a clinical pharmacist after climbing the corporate ladder for many years. Our family was a priority, and when her career began pulling her away from our family, she decided to walk away. She often said spending more time with me, my brother, and our dad was worth more than every penny she wasn't making. After taking a five-year sabbatical, she found another clinical pharmacist job where she's able to work from home and still honor her priorities.

I recently encountered a similar decision about stepping away from track for a season. So, I made a pro/con chart. The main pros were focusing on school, getting more sleep, having more time, avoiding burnout from running, and concentrating on my health. I had lost a lot of weight from running and was not eating enough to compensate. The only con was feeling like I was going to let down my teammates and coaches. The con weighed heavy on my shoulders, but I knew it would be best for my well-being if I took the season off. I knew my body could only take so much because I had been running six days a week for over two years.

After the fact, I'm glad I made this decision. I enjoyed a much-needed break from running. When cross country season rolled around, I felt refreshed and ready to start logging the miles again.

What big decisions are you facing? Using your heart and mind, weigh out the options, and pray hard. I'm sure you'll be able to make the best decision for you and others.

Reinforcements:

- Eliminate the dread by avoiding procrastination and tackling homework, and big projects head-on.

- A productive morning leads to a productive day.

- God, relationships, and health are a priority before work.

- Hard work apart from God is ambition. Hard work submitted unto God becomes worship.

- Pro/Con lists help us make an informed decision based on where our priorities lie.

Pause and Ponder:

1. Make a list of your top 10 priorities. Do any of these go against God's best for you?

_____

_____

_____

_____

2. Do you have a big decision you need to make soon? If so, make a pro/con list to aid in your decision-making.

Pros	Cons

8

MANAGING TIME

Idon't know about you, but I get overwhelmed at times. My teachers expect me to be a good student. My coaches expect me to be a good athlete. My community expects me to be a good citizen. My parents expect me to be a good kid.

We're pulled in multiple directions, and everywhere we turn, people expect us to give our best. If we're not careful, we'll wear ourselves thin and ultimately, snap. The key to avoiding this breaking point is appropriate time management. As mentioned in the previous chapter, we need to spend our time in a way that reflects what's most important to us.

TIME IS MONEY, OR IS IT?

We have our rich, and we have our poor. The amount of money varies from person to person. Time, on the other hand, does not change. While there's still breath in our bones, we all have twenty-four hours in a day, seven days in a week, and 365 days in a year. Except for leap year, of course.

We decide how we fill those hours, days, and years. Time is something non-refundable. We must carefully choose how we spend it. We can always make more money, but we'll never get back lost time without God's redemption, but that's a story for another day.

Speaking of stories, if you don't like how yours is going, start a new chapter today. Now's the time to make your story meaningful and impactful. Minimize the detours and rabbit trails. Avoid the excess fluff that wastes your time. Invest in what truly matters. Only then will you reap rewards that money can't buy.

THINK LONG-TERM

What do you love to do? Do you have a talent or skill you can harness and cultivate until you become an expert or guru in that area? What gets you excited about the future?

These are questions you need to ask yourself when planning your career path. Life is short, and we need to spend our time doing something we enjoy. In a YouTube video titled *This is How Terribly Short Your Life Is*, a 2017 study tested how well the American workforce likes their current job. The results were shocking. Eighty-five percent of workers say they dislike or hate their current job.[1]

We spend nearly a quarter of our lives in the workplace. How disappointing is it only fifteen percent like that part of their lives? Also, I wonder how being miserable twenty-five percent of the time spills over into the other seventy-five percent?

Let's you and I be part of the exception here. Let's not allow money to lead us down our career path, but rather let's allow our passion to lead us there. We don't need to waste our time doing things we don't enjoy, including a job we aren't passionate about. Even if the job offers twice the pay, it's not worth it!

QUALITY OVER QUANTITY

Have you ever sat down with your textbook to study, and after ten minutes of reading the material, you realize your mind was not processing the words because it was somewhere else? You may have spent ten minutes studying, but it didn't do you any good because you can't recall one thing you read.

It's not only the amount of time spent on a task, but also the quality of the time spent. To be effective, we want to be in the moment. I love a quote by Muhammad Ali which said, "Don't count the days, make the days count."[2]

I played the trombone for three years, and I learned the only way to get better is by playing difficult music for my current skill level. Unfortunately, practicing challenging music or rhythms are the only way to grow effectively. If my practice time was spent only on music I'd already mastered, I wouldn't improve—I'd be wasting my time.

Therefore, quality time is being in the moment. It's setting aside time to be productive. It's challenging yourself to promote growth. And it's doing something with a spirit of excellence.

PROCRASTINATION

We've all seen the sand in the hourglass slowly trickle down, and we know it will eventually all accumulate to the bottom. When the time's up, we have to look back and ask ourselves, *what did I accumulate?*

Time is precious. We must value and manage it well because time will run out before we know it.

While I'm not a procrastinator, I have seen the negative effects of procrastination from my peers. It's a bad habit that many of us must battle to overcome. The procrastinator always has the deadline or due date in mind. They think, *It's due in three days. I have plenty of time, so I'll do it later.*

They keep thinking they'll have time—until they don't. Then, they're stressed-out, morph into a workhorse, and pull an all-nighter the night

WE MUST REPLACE PROCRASTINATION WITH PROACTIVITY AND PACING.

before a project or assignment is due. Has this ever happened to you?

73

We must deliberately change our habits to overcome this. We must replace procrastination with proactivity and pacing.

The first step is to plan, plan, plan. Start by specifying your goals and defining how many hours it will take you to accomplish these goals. Then, make a schedule that's realistic to help you meet these goals. A planner is handy for this.

An important thing to stress here is we must be specific. Our goal isn't to pass the class. And honestly, it shouldn't necessarily be to ace the class either. Our goal should be to devote the time and energy necessary for us to learn the material and do the very best we possibly can.

Forbes, a well-known global media company who focuses on business and finance, explains the importance of making goals instead of resolutions. Studies have shown that less than twenty-five percent of people stay committed to their resolutions after thirty days, and only eight percent accomplish them.[3] That's disappointing!

The main reason for this failure is because resolutions tend to be vague and broad whereas goals are specific. It's easy to stop and lose focus when the result isn't well-defined. This defeats us on two fronts. First, it gives us a good excuse for when we fail. Secondly, it gives us an opportunity to fudge the results slightly enough to justify ourselves in accomplishing that resolution.

Nearly half of New Years' Resolutions in 2019 were health-related, such as *Exercise to get in shape* and *Diet to lose weight*.[4] Rather than saying this, we need to say, *I'm going to do thirty-minute workouts five days per week and eat 2,000 calories each day to lose ten pounds in ten weeks*. Do you see the difference?

The next tip for combating procrastination is to establish a reward system when meeting your goals. You must negotiate with yourself and say, *If I work now, I'll reward myself with (fill-in-the-blank) later*. Work isn't always fun, but it'll be more tolerable if we know there'll be an upcoming reward.

Resisting procrastination is important because we don't want to feel like we've lost control of the time. We rule circumstances. We don't let circumstances rule us. Not only does this create a stress-free zone, but we'll see higher quality work because we'll be well-rested and on our A-game.

A bonus is knowing you're doing something productive you would've otherwise needed to do later. That's motivating in itself. Once you break out of the habit of procrastination, you'll never put off for tomorrow what you can do today.

THE UNPREDICTABLE FUTURE

Life is unpredictable, and there can be hundreds of things that pop-up. It's important to expect the unexpected because the unexpected is sometimes inevitable. Obstacles pop up out of nowhere, and unexpected delays slow us down. Without considering these setbacks, we tend to overestimate how much time we have available to do something.

When planning, especially something important, accommodate time for the unforeseen. You never know when life's going to throw you a curveball.

Say you've planned a date with a person you really like. Wouldn't you rather wait in your car for a few minutes than show up late and flustered? What if you planned to be there five minutes early, but something unplanned occurred, such as unexpected traffic? No worries, mate! You're right on-time looking cool, calm, and collected. You can thank me later.

DO ONLY WHAT YOU CAN HANDLE

While tempting, we shouldn't take on more than we can handle. Although difficult and perhaps awkward, we need to be okay saying no sometimes.

I know firsthand about people-pleasing and, in doing so, have agreed to take on things I didn't have extra time for. That doesn't do them or me any favors.

Managing time is impossible when we have no time to execute. Let's flip the switch on overestimating and underdelivering. Instead, let's work on underestimating the time we have available to work on a task and then overdeliver on the final product. Remember, it's not about quantity. It's about quality.

TIMELINE YOUR TO-DO LIST

I write down anything noteworthy to get it off my chest. I write down due dates, passwords, short and long-term goals, what I plan to do each day, and tasks I need to get done. My planner is beneficial for this. We've already talked about prioritizing your to-do list, but timelining your list allows you to respect deadlines, remember important information at the right time, and make goals while tracking your progress.

When things get stressful, I estimate the amount of time it'll take for me to complete each task and note it in my planner next to the task. This helps me maintain realistic expectations, so I don't over plan the day. Even if I don't get everything done for that day, I carry it over to the next day until I complete it.

Being an avid to-do lister has contributed to my growth and success in high school. Not only do I worry a lot less, but it also allows me to remember things better simply because I've written them down.

Sure, I could make notes or reminders on my phone, but there's something special for me about physically writing that releases internal tension. Plus, it's much more satisfying to cross out something I've finished. It makes it tangible and very rewarding.

Furthermore, I've found the reminders on my phone often defeat the purpose of saving time. I'm one click away from accessing the world at my fingertips—don't tell me that isn't tempting. Getting side-tracked is easy. How many times do we get hacked by text messages, a game, or social media when we should be working? More times than I'd like to admit.

Always stay focused on the main thing. When you complete one thing, move on to the next thing. Being able to manage time won't guarantee success, but it'll improve your chances. Many young people haven't developed this skill, and you'll be a step ahead if you learn to manage your time wisely.

Reinforcements:

- Focus more on the quality of time invested rather than the quantity of time spent.

- Time is nonrefundable, so wisely choose how you'll spend it.

- Resisting procrastination helps us rule circumstances rather than circumstances ruling us.

- Plan for the unpredictable with a time cushion.

- Reflect your priorities with your time. Always stay focused on the main thing.

Pause and Ponder:

1. Make a to-do list of five things you need to accomplish over the next week with an estimated time of completion.

   _____

   _____

   _____

   _____

2. What's something you could do today that you're putting off for tomorrow?

   _____

   _____

   _____

   _____

9

MINIMIZING STRESS

*"Cast your burden upon the LORD, and He will sustain you;
He will never allow the righteous to be shaken"
(Psalm 55:22).*

I hate to say it, but stress is unavoidable. The teen years especially are full of difficult experiences that can result in stress overload. The effects of stress are harmful. It negatively affects our health, well-being, and mood if we don't learn to manage it well. There are ways to minimize and contain stress, so we don't do something we'll regret later.

UNCOVERING THE ROOT CAUSE

Stress can come from several factors. The key to managing stress is to get to the root by asking ourselves, *What's the true reason for my stress?*

It can come from feeling overwhelmed, fear of not measuring up, or loss of control. Often, it results from us putting too much pressure on ourselves. So instead of taking a chill pill, what if we tried taking a load off first?

Sometimes, the root can come from past hurts. Sometimes, it can come from an unfortunate or overwhelming situation. Stress is contagious, and sometimes we catch it from other people we hang around. Whatever it may be, you must attack the root to combat the stress you feel.

The root may be deep and difficult to cut out, but once it's removed, it removes the problem permanently, not temporarily. Then, we need to be careful not to plant seeds anymore.

I know I'm not alone when I say I hate giving a presentation in front of the class. I always feel stressed, so much so I can feel my paper shaking in my hands. I've learned the root of that stress comes from the fear of judgment by my peers. Why do we care so much about what others think? The truth is *their opinions of me don't change me*. I am who I am, and the more secure I am in that, the influence others have over me lessens. I've improved, but I can still be very self-conscious at times. Recognizing the root has helped me a ton.

We need to realize, in presentations and life, most people around you are honestly thinking of their presentations and their issues instead of you and yours. Or they'll compare your presentation to one they already gave. Right? We can be so self-centered.

We feel like everyone is watching us when truthfully, almost everyone is only concerned with themselves and their problems. Figuring this out also helped me become a lot less nervous.

It's All in What You Make It

While this is way easier said than done, what if we trained ourselves to go with the flow? I'm not talking about morally or socially but rather adapting to circumstances and embracing change. What if we replaced rigidity with flexibility? Not getting worked up over situations requires significant patience.

We can't always control the situation, but we can control how we react to it. Charles Swindoll wrote, "I'm convinced that life is 10% what happens to me and 90% how I react to it."[1] Have you ever worked yourself up over something, maybe your class presentation, and then afterward think, *Well, that wasn't so bad.* I've learned that we typically perceive a situation much worse than it is.

When I get stressed, my mom constantly reminds me that circumstance is a matter of perspective; it's all in what you make it. *Whether I wake up and say I'm going to have a great day or a horrible day, I'm often correct.* This isn't only because of the circumstances I encounter, but it's because of how I react to those circumstances.

Having a positive outlook, even through difficulty, is incredibly challenging. Sometimes, when it rains, it pours, and it's hard to see the sunshine from all the rain clouds. But I guarantee by looking around a little bit deeper, you'll find something positive to celebrate. What you're looking for may not be on the surface or obvious, but because you don't see it, doesn't mean it isn't there.

> WE CAN TRUST GOD TO WORK ALL THINGS TOGETHER FOR OUR GOOD. EVEN IF IT DOESN'T LOOK LIKE IT AT THE MOMENT. GOD'S ULTIMATE PLAN WILL NEVER BE THWARTED.

The rain cleanses the earth and brings life into dry places. We can trust God to work all things together for our good. Even if it doesn't look like it at the moment. God's ultimate plan will never be thwarted. So, don't stress. Trust! Would you agree?

STAYING RELAXED

Stress activates our fight or flight system. We don't always need to run away, nor do we always need to fight. To manage our stress, we must learn practical relaxation techniques. So, what are some good relaxation techniques we can incorporate?

Deep breathing is helpful and simple enough. Slowly breathe in through your nose and out through your mouth. This slows your heart rate and lowers blood pressure.

Also, I like meditating on God's word. Find several scriptures in the Bible to give you hope and peace, and memorize them.

Then, when stressful situations arise, you can bring these verses to memory, and it will renew your mind and your strength.

Journaling is another technique I enjoy. I find writing everything on my mind down on paper allows me to perform a mental dump. Then, I can prioritize and organize or delete it if it's not essential. In addition, I no longer feel the stress of having to remember it once it's written down.

Connecting with others has also been proven to reduce stress. While human physical interaction is on the decline, stress levels are continuing to increase. Surprisingly, the simple act of talking face-to-face with another human can trigger hormones that relieve stress when you're feeling agitated or insecure. So, put away the electronics and find a hang-out buddy.

Exercise is one of the primary methods I use to relieve stress. According to the Mayo Clinic, people who exercise reported less stress than those who didn't. Exercise produces endorphins, a feel-good neurotransmitter.

Mayo likens exercise to *meditation in motion*. Not only does exercise release mental stress, but it promotes full-body health by decreasing diseases and making it easier to control weight. Rhythmic, cardio activities such as walking, running, swimming, and dancing deem to be some of the most effective forms of stress-releasing exercise.[2]

I can testify to the effectiveness of running as a stress reliever. School is overwhelming at times, and after a stressful day of school, a run around the track a few times helps me clear my mind of worry. It also re-energizes my body and improves my focus.

Stress can produce muscle tension, which causes stiff and achy muscles in the upper body, including the neck and jaw. In cross country races, my face tenses when the pain starts to kick. I didn't even realize it until my coach told me. Flexing my facial muscles wastes energy and leads the rest of my body to tense up as well. To avoid this, I take deep breaths, relax my hands, and occasionally shake out my arms.

Everyone deals with stress differently, and some worse than others. Experiment and find out what stress-relievers work best for you. We all should develop a way to manage stress. Make it something you enjoy doing to get your mind off your anxieties. Once you find a way to handle your stress, it will allow you to stay calm through intense situations in school or at home.

Reinforcements:

- Stress can negatively affect our health, well-being, and mood if we don't learn to manage it well.

- Get to the root of the stress to conquer it.

- Circumstance is a matter of perspective; it's all in what you make it.

- To manage our stress, we must learn effective relaxation techniques.

Pause and Ponder:

1. Thinking of your biggest stressor, what do you think the root of it is?

   _____

   _____

   _____

   _____

2. What relaxation techniques can you incorporate into your daily schedule?

   _____

   _____

   _____

10

RESTING PROPERLY

Would you agree many teens undervalue rest? Physical rest and sleep are crucial, but I've also found short mental breaks to be equally important.

Sleep deprivation affects me on many levels. It becomes hard to focus, and I develop headaches and find myself in a bad mood. I also notice my performance in school is negatively affected. Can you relate?

Knowing even God took the seventh day to rest made me start to value rest more. If God rested, then we, as imperfect beings, definitely need a day to regain our focus and energy. It's so important because honoring the Sabbath through rest made God's top-ten list.

FINDING BALANCE IN REST

Like all practices, the key is balance. I've mentioned the adverse effects of not getting enough rest. However, resting too much is also a problem. A couple of hours of personal downtime per day is usually a good thing. On the other hand, spending half the day on the couch binging Netflix every day is harmful.

Have you heard of the two-day rule when trying a new activity? To stay committed to something, we can follow this rule by not taking two consecutive days off. I could run seven days per week, and there were times when I did. Unfortunately, I learned the hard way I must take a day off to avoid injury and optimize my performance. But I also learned if I take a couple of days off in a row, it's more tempting to take a third, fourth, and so on until I'm no longer consistently pursuing my goal.

Our brains are good at making excuses, arguing that we deserve more rest than we need. I encourage you to find the balance right for you. Plan your week on a calendar, keeping in mind the two-day rule, and don't be hesitant to schedule in some daily downtime and a rest day each week.

CONTROVERSIAL CORRELATION BETWEEN SUCCESS AND REST

My mind still tries to believe rest is bad and only for the weak and lazy. I heard a motivational speaker, whose YouTube video has over five million views say, "If you're going to be successful, you have to be willing to give up sleep. If you go to sleep, you might miss the opportunity to be successful."[1]

I realize he was extreme to make a point. However, for those individuals who're highly disciplined and willing to do anything to be successful, this method is dangerous. I'm sure he was aiming high to hit low, meaning he says to give up sleep, but he's hoping people will at least cut their current sleep pattern short a couple of hours. Regardless, I'd never do that to you. I'll give it like I want to take it—straight up honest.

To succeed, you don't need to go days without eating and sleeping. *You don't need to obsess for success.* What you do need is rest and balance.

SLEEPING CONSISTENTLY

A part of proper rest is developing a somewhat consistent and appropriate sleep schedule. I'm sure you're aware, the teenage years are some of the most crucial years of physical growth and development. According to the National Sleep Foundation, teens fourteen to seventeen years old need an average of eight to ten hours of sleep per night.[2] I recommend experimenting and finding out what works for you.

Consistency is key. For me, I try to avoid staying up late. When I do, I wake up later the next morning and then I don't get tired until later the following evening. Before I know it, I've found myself in a bad sleep cycle. Ever wonder why Mondays are so hard? This may be a good clue.

I challenge you to consistently hit your sleep goals and see how it changes your productivity. The hardest part

> QUALITY SLEEP CYCLES ESTABLISH THE FRAMEWORK FOR SUCCESS.

will be the first couple of days, but once you develop a good habit, it's much easier to sustain. Quality sleep cycles establish the framework for success.

As teens, it's easy to develop a bad sleep cycle. Electronics are mainly to blame, so we need to be disciplined to shut them down when needed. According to the National Sleep Foundation, the more time a person spends on electronic devices in the evening, the harder it is for them to fall asleep or stay asleep.[3] A good substitution is reading a good book.

DON'T SNOOZE

We all know the saying, "You snooze, you lose." It means if you wait or are indecisive, or aren't paying attention, you'll miss a great opportunity. This is a good philosophy to follow, so don't hit the snooze button.

Rise and shine, pumpkin! If you think you need five more minutes, set your alarm accordingly. Take the first opportunity of the day to conquer your feelings and hit the ground running.

Sometimes, it only takes one productive decision to lead to another.

I love American comedian Demetri Martin's, take on it. He says, "If you really think about it, hitting the snooze button in the morning doesn't even make sense. It's like saying, 'I hate getting up in the morning. So, I do it over... and over... and over again.'"[4]

I challenge you to resist the urge. Successful people don't roll-over. Instead, they're already on a roll first thing in the morning. And they do it day after day after day. Once you figure this one out, you'll be glad you did!

REST IN THE BIBLE

As mentioned in the chapter-opening, the Bible instructs us to remember the Sabbath and make it holy. It's one of the Ten Commandments. We need rest so we're not carried away by the flow of the world.

I heard some wise advice from Jeff Pratt, author of *The Homeward Call*, who said, "Sometimes, it takes slowing down to catch up with God." In a world that runs on supersonic speed, we often run out ahead of the One who should be leading us. God has big plans for our life, but sometimes we can't hear this voice directing us because it's blocked out by a chaotic world. The word tells us His yoke is easy, and His burden is light. When we're always on the go, a lot of our actions become striving instead of abiding.

When we strive, we produce by our hard work. A simpler and easier way is abiding. In John 15:5, Jesus says, *"I am the vine, you are the branches; he who abides in Me and I in him, he bears much fruit."* Think about it. The branch doesn't strain to produce fruit, but the fruit comes forth simply because the branch is attached to the vine. When we abide in the Vine, Jesus, we deliver from a place of peace and rest, and our fruit is much tastier. Do you see the difference?

Every day, we need to pause our work and reflect on Jesus. This will re-focus our aim, so our labor isn't in vain. It also adjusts our perspective. I'm less likely to get stressed out when I'm centered on Jesus.

I admit, this is a challenge for me, and my mind often wanders when I'm supposed to be contemplating on the Lord. It's an art, and I'll continue to practice it.

What if, instead of watching the world on social media to see what they're doing, we traded that time to look for Jesus to see what He's doing? I'd rather join Him and *His* efforts than the world in theirs. I'm up for the challenge. How about you?

LESS CAN BE MORE

Another thing I struggle with is balance, and that's interesting because I talk about it a lot. After getting serious with running, I wanted to be the best I could possibly be. I always thought the more work you put in, the more you get out. Sounds logical, right?

However, there have been studies to disprove this idea, including a study from Stanford University. Economics professor, John Pencavel, found productivity per hour declines sharply when a person works more than fifty hours a week. After fifty-five hours, productivity drops so much that putting in any more hours would be pointless. Those who work up to seventy hours a week are only getting the same amount of work done as those who put in the fifty-five hours.[5]

I experimented with this theory by decreasing my weekly mileage. Surprisingly, I found when decreasing my weekly mileage goals by taking Sunday off, my times seemed to improve. Crazy, huh?

I've learned that no matter how driven you are, you'll eventually drive yourself out of gas if you don't take time to refuel. The highest performance cars require the highest octane of gas to refuel properly. While this comes at a higher price, it's necessary for the car to continue to perform at a high level. If you put regular gas in a premium required car, it can damage the engine, leading to reduced performance and fuel economy.[6]

No matter how hard-working, dedicated, or mentally strong you may be, you must take time to refuel by setting aside quality time to rest. If not, you'll eventually be less productive and efficient. You might even experience more stress and quicker exhaustion.

> I'VE LEARNED THAT NO MATTER HOW DRIVEN YOU ARE, YOU'LL EVENTUALLY DRIVE YOURSELF OUT OF GAS IF YOU DON'T TAKE TIME TO REFUEL.

Exercise scientists measured heart rate to see what form of exercise burned the most calories. They studied aerobic cardio versus high-intensity interval training (HIIT). Aerobic cardio included activity at the same intensity throughout the entire workout with no rest. HIIT, on the other hand, included short bursts of intense exercise followed by short rest repeated several times without allowing the heart rate to decrease significantly. While many other factors can determine which form of exercise is the best, calories burned is typically the most used indicator. The data proved that HIIT (with rest) burned more calories than aerobic cardio in the same timeframe.

It's more about the quality of time spent rather than the amount of time spent. HIIT workouts were shorter, but because the intensity was higher quality, it was more effective. Denzel Washington sums it up well. "Just because you are doing a lot more doesn't mean you are getting a lot more done."[7]

Anyone who's done a vigorous activity knows that taking a break helps. It decreases your physical fatigue, renews your energy, and allows you to mentally prepare so you can perform with more efficiency when you return.

REST IN AGRICULTURE

Agriculture is another great example of the importance of rest. Typically, farmers have four sections of soil dedicated to growing certain types of crops. The four sections include legumes: to grow crops like beans, peas, and potatoes; roots: to grow crops

like onions, beets, and carrots; fruits: to grow crops like toma-
toes, melons, and squash; and leaves: to grow crops like lettuce,
spinach, and corn.

Before crop rotation was popularized in the 1730s by Charles
Townshend, farmers used all the plots of land to grow crops.
Makes sense, right? If you've got it, why not invest it all?

This method was used much less after the benefits of crop
rotation were discovered. Charles Townshend allowed one plot
of land to rest for a period to regain its nutrients until the next
season and also rotated each type of crop in a pattern to a new
kind of soil.

Essentially, each growing season, he closed off a different section to recycle its nutrients while rotating another kind of crop
to be grown in the other sections. He discovered crop rotation
increases crop yield and soil fertility while reducing soil erosion
and weeds.

After Townshend's results were shared, crop rotation was
increasingly practiced by farmers. By the 19th century, most
farmers practiced crop rotation because of its proven benefits.[8]

The revolution produced a surplus of food and has been a
large factor contributing to feeding the exponential population
growth from one billion people in 1804, to reach seven billion
people in 2012.[9]

We're no different. We must periodically step away from our
craft and regain our energy, to continue with increased yield,
productivity, and strength.

MENTAL BREAKS

No matter what you're doing, brain breaks are needed. After a
few minutes rest, you'd be surprised at how much it will improve
your attention span. Even while writing this, I try not to write
for greater than an hour at a time. Not that I view this as work,
but I do this so I can make sure I'm providing you with the best
quality content possible. Even taking ten to twenty minutes of
break makes a huge difference. After taking a short break from

writing, I seem to get a new perspective. Feeling rejuvenated, I return ready to resume my journey as fresh ideas pop into my head.

I hope you see mental rest is as important as physical rest. We all need to find what we like to do that requires little thought and no stress. I bet you this is the first self-help book that's encouraging you to watch some TV every day. Within reason, I see nothing wrong with spending time solely doing an unproductive activity to take a break from a chaotic and restless world.

The most common ways people use to decompress their minds are listening to music, watching TV shows, reading books, watching online videos, listening to podcasts, taking a walk, writing, and meditating. One isn't better than the other, but I do believe whatever calms your mind and relieves your worries the most is the best one for you. For me, every night before bed, I put away all work and relax. The primary way I currently find mental rest is by watching some TV with my family, listening to audiobooks, or reading my Bible.

Reinforcements:

- Rest brings balance to our lives, so we don't obsess for success.

- According to the National Sleep Foundation, teens between the ages of fourteen to seventeen years old need an average of eight to ten hours of sleep per night.

- Resist the snooze button. Don't rollover. Roll out.

- When we abide in the Vine, Jesus, we produce from a place of peace and rest.

- No matter how driven you are, you'll eventually drive yourself out of gas if you don't take time to refuel.

- Mental breaks improve your attention span.

Pause and Ponder:

1. On a scale of 1 to 10, how do you rate your work/rest balance?

| 1 | 2 | 3 | 4 | 5 | 6 | 7 | 8 | 9 | 10 |

All work, ◯ ◯ ◯ ◯ ◯ ◯ ◯ ◯ ◯ ◯ All play,
No play   No work

2. With a goal being 5, what are some ways you can improve your number?

_____

_____

_____

_____

11

HANDLING ADDICTION

When you can stop, you don't want to. When you want to stop, you can't. First appearing small, manageable, and harmless, addictions grow until they become difficult to escape. Sometimes, they're obvious, but often the addict doesn't realize they have a problem.

The fact of the matter is—I've been addicted without even realizing it.

Before you gasp, let's define addiction. Merriam-Webster states that an addiction is a compulsive, chronic, physiological, or psychological need for a habit-forming substance, behavior, or activity having harmful physical, psychological, or social effects and typically causing well-defined symptoms (such as anxiety, irritability, tremors, or nausea) upon withdrawal or abstinence.[1] You see, addiction doesn't have to be to a chemical substance. It's a strong inclination to do, use, or indulge in anything repeatedly.

Did you notice habit-forming in that definition? I can't stress enough how important it is to develop good habits and break bad ones. We're creatures of habit. Addiction feeds into this, drawing us physiologically or psychologically into its clutches. We repeatedly go back for more, again and again, no matter the consequences. Addictions must meet two criteria. It must be something beyond our control and outside the realm of reasonable use. And it must be impacting your life in some negative way.

Have you ever felt anxious over forgetting your cell phone, like a piece of you is missing? Do video games interfere with fulfilling daily responsibilities, cause social withdrawal or sleep disturbances? Do you spend excessive amounts of time thinking about food, overindulge at mealtime, feel guilty about eating, or hide your food? If you answered yes to any of these, you might have a problem.

In 2009, addiction expert Scott Gallagher conducted a survey to define the top twelve teen addictions. Here are his findings.[2]

- Junk food

- Internet/computer use

- Marijuana

- Alcohol

- Tobacco

- Sugar/candy

- Overeating

- Under-eating/anorexia

- Self-harm (primarily cutting behavior)

- Sex

- Bullying or abusing others

- Video games

CLASH OF THE WILL

At this point, I suppose you're wondering what my addiction was. Unfortunately, I've struggled with a couple of different things. In my preteen years, a game called Clash of Clans pretty much dictated my life for about two years, and my life became extremely imbalanced. The game was worked to create a fixation because, to make progress, you must continually stay engaged. Otherwise, your whole clan suffers.

I enjoyed playing it and became really good at it. After acceptance into one of the best war clans in the United States, I became even more obsessive because I didn't want them to kick me out for being inactive. When I wasn't playing, I was thinking about it, strategizing next moves and countermoves. I played it pretty much all day for a whole summer, going into sixth grade.

My mom tried to help me find balance by setting time restrictions and enforcing breaks, but it was summer, and we weren't consistent with it. After I told her I was dreaming about Clash of Clans, she encouraged me to take drastic measures. I decided to quit entirely and deleted my two-year account to break the addiction. It was extremely hard that first week. I almost felt sick, deleting all that progress, and I became anxious about my newly found free time. But the following week was easier. When I found freedom and the game no longer consumed me, I felt so much better, my thoughts were clearer, and I never considered redownloading the game.

ANOTHER DOWNWARD SPIRAL

Fast forward to my eighth grade and freshman year of high school. I had joined cross country, and to be fast, we were instructed to be as lean as possible. Our coaches encouraged us to cut out all soda and minimize sugar. As a disciplined individual, I took this too far and counted every calorie I ate, thinking that losing weight was the answer to running faster. Shortly thereafter, I developed body image issues, which progressed to an eating disorder.

Eating extremely low-calorie and running massive mileage, I lost more and more weight. Satan attacked me with this mental illness. I looked in the mirror and at five feet, ten inches tall and 115 pounds, thought I was fat.

This eating disorder took me through several stages. Next, came a cycle of binging and starving. I restricted my food consumption throughout the day, but right before bed, I'd start with a small snack, perhaps one spoonful of peanut butter. Then, one led to another and another. I felt like I couldn't stop because I was so malnourished from under-eating all day. Next thing I knew, I had eaten a half jar of peanut butter.

This became a daily occurrence. I was so disappointed in myself after binging, feeling awful, shameful, and way too full. Thus, the next day I cut calories and sometimes worked out extra to compensate for my binge. But the following night, the same thing would happen again. Thankfully, I didn't become bulimic, but this cycle of binging and starving was terrible, and food was an obsession.

I'm so glad I've found freedom in how I view and consume food. It took me walking away from running a season of track, keeping a food journal to ensure enough calorie consumption throughout the day, regular weigh-ins, a lot of in-your-face truth talk, and being held accountable by my parents. Oh, and lots of prayers.

Unlike Clash of Clans, I couldn't merely eliminate food. It's much more complicated than simply *stop and eat normal*. Food addiction is a mental illness. I had to view food differently, and I had to change the way I saw myself. Reading the Bible definitely helped me renew my way of thinking. Sometimes, I still struggle, digging up those old mindsets again. But I've come a long way in finding balance and freedom in this area.

THE LURE

Addictions often result from stress or emotional pain and are likened to a form of self-medication, usually providing a short-term reward like stress-relief or happiness. Common factors resulting in addiction range from family history, to depression or anxiety, to negative social experiences or self-esteem issues.[3]

Sadly, our adversary Satan puts a huge target on teens because of our vulnerability and enormous potential. He whispers thoughts in our head, which makes us feel an uncontrollable desire for something we don't need. He's the author of confusion and the source of feelings of fear, anxiety, shame, and unworthiness.

> SADLY, OUR ADVERSARY SATAN PUTS A HUGE TARGET ON TEENS BECAUSE OF OUR VULNERABILITY AND ENORMOUS POTENTIAL.

The enemy's greatest weapon is the power of suggestion. He'll tell you *Only one time,* and *It won't hurt anyone,* and *No one will ever know.* The enemy will come to you disguised as something you've always wanted. 2 Corinthians 11:14 says, *"And no wonder, for even Satan disguises himself as an angel of light."*

If we walk in the light, we will expose all darkness and uncover his schemes before they take root. If we can learn to live based on our beliefs no matter the circumstance, we'll become righteous warriors. Our feelings won't rule us, and neither will that voice of temptation in our head.

It's best to nip it in the bud before the poisonous flower of addiction blossoms. But what if it's too late? What if you're already trapped in its vicious cycle? Then I implore you to seek help, immediately. At the end of this book, there are some resources for you to turn to for help.

I've mentioned my experience with video game and food addictions. Now, I'll briefly discuss a couple more of the top addictions teens may struggle with throughout the remainder of this chapter. This information by no means, however, should replace seeking professional help.

CELL PHONE ADDICTION

The largest percent of non-substance addiction is cell phone use, which is reported to release similar addictive neurotransmitters to your brain like drugs and alcohol.

Cell phone addiction in teens has risen to an all-time high. According to results of a 2016 Common Sense Media Report, an astonishing 50% of teens admit to being addicted to their smartphones.[4] Addiction to electronics results in several micro-interruptions throughout the day. According to the New York Post, new research concluded that Americans check their phones on average once every twelve minutes—burying their heads in their phones eighty times a day.[5] Other studies have linked unhappiness to cell phone use. There's indisputable evidence stating that excessive electronic use is harmful. However, we continue to solidify the addiction to science because we still use them.

When you look around at people in lines, waiting rooms, or restaurants, everyone is on their electronic device. We don't socialize like we used to. It's almost as if we avoid the stillness of being left with our thoughts or the pleasures of having a conversation with others. I want to propose this is why the average human's attention span has decreased from thirteen seconds to eight seconds from 2000 to 2013. Did you know this is a shorter attention span than a goldfish?[6]

I know I can relate. When I watch educational videos on YouTube for school, I usually put the speed on 1.5X or 2X because I have a hard time focusing for an extended period of time. It would be nice if I could do that to my teachers. Haha! I don't want fluff or small talk. Give me what I need to know, and let's go! I could cut the school day in half.

We're addicted to fast solutions and immediate gratifications with our smartphones. We have the world at our fingertips. Google will take you anywhere you want to go and tell you anything you want to know. Furthermore, rewards, such as texts, likes, and social media updates trigger a dopamine release signaling the pleasure center of our brain.

Technology addiction expert, Dr. David Greenfield, refers to smartphones as *the world's smallest slot machine* because they operate on a variable reinforcement schedule. "Every once in a while, you get a reward... a piece of information, a text, an email, an update... but you don't know when you're going to get it, what it's going to be and how good it's going to be."[7] This is the same reinforcement schedule as a slot machine to a gambler. What's highly addictive about these things is the idea and the neurobiological expectation they set up that a reward is coming, but you don't know when you're going to get it.

So how do you know if you have an addiction to your smart-phone? Here are some symptoms identified by PsychGuides.com:[8]

- Increased Tolerance: Needing more time on your phone, new apps, or the latest technology to get your fix.

- Excessive use: Characterized by loss sense of time and impulsive, frequent, constant checking of your cell phone.

- Persistent failed attempts to use your cell phone less often.

- Withdrawal: Feeling ill at ease or anxious when you're away from your phone.

- Mood Altering: Using technology to alter your mood or change your state of mind.

- Relationships, work, or responsibilities suffer due to excessive cell phone use.

This doesn't include eye strain, neck tension, and sleep disturbances, also caused by excessive cell phone use.

UNPLUGGING

So, what's the solution? Do we throw our phones away and go back to the dark ages? I don't think we have to go that far. Cell phones can be healthy and useful when used in the right context and at appropriate times. Again, it's about finding balance.

Let's discuss some simple solutions to get you pointed in the right direction. First, establish screen-free zones. Put your cell phone away at mealtimes, family outings, and social gatherings. Learn to be present more and live in the moment. Make relationships priority. Also, keep your cell phone out of the bedroom at night to prevent sleep disturbance and insomnia.

Another suggestion is to outsmart your smartphone by downloading apps, such as BreakFree, designed to monitor and curb your phone usage.

Taking simple steps towards decreasing the time you spend on your cell phone can be a gamechanger. I've found that turning off notifications and using the Do Not Disturb mode have helped me decrease my cell phone use. Also, I monitor my screen time mode found under settings on my iPhone to get a reality check of the actual time I spend on my device.

The key is awareness. Know how much time you're spending on your phones, how it affects you physically and emotionally, how it affects your relationships, and whether your responsibilities are negatively affected. Once you're aware, you can mindfully break your addiction.

SUBSTANCE ADDICTION

Substance addictions affect teenagers from every social and economic status. Overwhelmingly, one in five teens admit to recreational drug use, and when asked why, they most commonly reply, "to fit in."[9] Unfortunately, ease of access is also a top response. Adderall, inhalants, marijuana, opioids, benzodiazepines, and anabolic steroids are some of the most commonly abused drugs among teens.

It's important to know the difference between drug abuse and addiction and equally important to know neither are good. Teen drug abuse can have long-term cognitive and behavioral effects since the teenage brain is still developing.[10] It's best to avoid drugs altogether.

> TEEN DRUG ABUSE CAN HAVE LONG-TERM COGNITIVE AND BEHAVIORAL EFFECTS SINCE THE TEENAGE BRAIN IS STILL DEVELOPING.[10]

Sadly, teenagers addicted to substances rely on that substance to feel good, to have fun, and to bury their misery. However, these substances will never leave you fulfilled or satisfied. The only one who can truly bring you complete freedom and fulfillment is Jesus Christ.

Four years ago, I attended the funeral of a relative who died from a heroin overdose. She was thirty-six years old. I listened as my mom described a beautiful young girl who was full of life—adventurous and a little mischievous. Yet, as I looked at her body lying in the casket, I could see the destruction her addiction had caused. A beautiful life—stolen.

Countless lives have been destroyed because of drugs. Substance addiction is like signing a contract with the enemy, giving him years of your life, lots of money, and your mental state in exchange for a temporary high or escape. More than 70,200 Americans died from drug overdoses in 2017, including illicit drugs and prescription opioids—a two-fold increase in a decade.[11] That is over twice the population of the city I live in![12]

The bottom line is, don't get hooked on substances. Don't even try them. Experimenting with drugs is like playing with fire. I had a great friend who was happy, outgoing, and smart. But when he got into drug abuse, it changed his character. His grades dropped, he started hanging with the wrong crowd, and now it seems he can't help but to live for the next high. It's so sad.

All of us have so much potential. Addiction holds us back from so much, including our relationship with the Lord. It isn't worth sacrificing the future only to feel short bursts of artificial happiness followed by a crash, which requires larger amounts to achieve the next high. A relationship with God is lasting happiness, a river that never dries up, a fire that doesn't stop burning. Choose life before it's too late.

If you struggle with substance addiction or abuse, please find professional help immediately. Again, I've placed resources and numbers in the back pages of this book you can turn to for help.

FINDING A FREEDOM THAT LASTS

Breaking addictions is hard because we have to make ourselves more conscious of the decisions we make. We have to initiate the change. We have to seek help.

Addictions are bad habits gone really bad. They're from the enemy who comes to steal, kill, and destroy your life and relationships. The key to handling addiction is to commit to seeking professional help and staying the course. When you fail, pick yourself up and try again. You can find freedom, and you can do hard things!

The first step to freedom is embracing the truth—no matter how much it hurts. Through my own experiences, addiction is hard to overcome. It's possible, but it's hard.

Addiction is like being on a small ship controlled by a mighty whirlpool. The easiest way to escape is in the beginning when the ship is on the outer ring of the current. As time progresses, the current gets stronger, and your downward spiral becomes near impossible to escape unless there's outside help to pull you out. If there's no outsider, the feelings of helplessness increase, and we begin to accept the fate of our downfall.

Something small and unmonitored can grow, becoming a large monster that controls your life before you know it. If you notice any of these tendencies, please find help. Confide in a trusted adult. My parents really helped me win my battles. I have faith that you can win your battles, too.

Reinforcements:

- Addiction is never good and always holds us back from reaching our full potential.

- Addictions often result from stress or emotional pain and are likened to a form of self-medication, usually providing a short-term reward like relief from stress or happiness.

- According to results of a 2016 Common Sense Media Report, an astonishing 50% of teens admit to being addicted to their smartphones.

- Cellphones are like the world's smallest slot machines because of the neurobiological expectation they set up that a reward is coming, but you don't know when you're going to get it.

- Teen drug abuse can have long-term cognitive and behavioral effects since the teenage brain is still developing.

- Self-honesty is necessary to break an addiction.

- If you struggle with addiction, please seek professional help.

Pause and Ponder:

1. What addiction(s), if any, do you struggle with?

2. What do you need in order to find freedom? Who can you reach out to for help?

3. What's holding you back from seeking freedom right now?

_____

_____

_____

_____

12

DODGING THE COMPARISON TRAP

Comparison is an easy trap to fall in. With access to social media, we compare everything from looks, wealth, accomplishments, status, skills, and friends more than ever before. The enemy works overtime in this arena, feeding us lies like *you're not good enough, and you don't have enough, and you don't offer enough.*

The wise Theodore Roosevelt famously quoted, "Comparison is the thief of joy."[1] How true it is. We can never be fully content with what God has provided for us while constantly looking at what He's given everyone else.

Comparison can affect anyone. Interestingly, the world's elitist—those who've everything—are often the most discontent because they fear someone will outdo them. They're always looking down upon the rising ranks of the second, third, and fourth place in an effort to preserve their throne.

SATISFACTION KILLER

If we all compared our accomplishments, none of us would be satisfied. We'd try to one-up one another instead of striving to reach our full potential. Instead of seeking to be respected and revered by others, we should do what God has called us to do and focus on pleasing Him. In the end, the only opinion that matters will be His.

I like to go to the gym and lift weights from time to time. As a runner, I'm weaker than most guys there, especially upper body. Like any guy, I don't want to appear weak when I'm benching 130 pounds, and the guys next to me are benching 250 pounds. Heck, I bet you just compared your bench to mine without even thinking twice. This is something we all need to work on.

> IN THE END, THE ONLY OPINION THAT MATTERS WILL BE HIS.

I had to get out of my head and open my eyes. When I did, I discovered this perception was far from the truth. These guys didn't care about me. They were focused on their workout. They came to better themselves, not criticize me and my workout.

The truth of the matter is, I don't want to be their size. As a distance runner, that would be detrimental. Also, that would be me trying to be someone else, not who I'm created to be. If I'm watching them and concerned about what they think, then I'm not the best me.

Wouldn't you agree, we're all on different levels with different goals in mind? We should never criticize those working hard and giving effort. And if someone criticizes you while you're attempting something, even if you mess up, then they're the one with problems—not you. Making fun of someone at the gym is like making fun of an addict in a rehab facility.

I've learned to be okay with not being good at everything. This example may sound ridiculous to you, but at some point in your life, I bet you'll experience something similar. If comparison is a struggle for you, my advice is to keep your eyes forward. Focus on *your* goal. If your eyes do roam, let it be to encourage others and cheer them on. But don't let them steal your joy. Guard yourself against both jealousy and pride.

THE NEVER ENOUGH MENTALITY

With almost eight billion people in this world, there will always be someone better, stronger, smarter, and prettier, or more handsome. A *be the best* expectation is simply unachievable. And it will always leave us never feeling good enough.

During the last indoor track season, the pitfalls of comparison invaded my life. The last meet had arrived, and I was super thrilled to run a personal record-breaking five-minute mile with a time of 4:59.59. Being in the *sub 5 club* was something I wanted to be a part of, kind of like upgrading your silver Madden player to gold.

My joy seemed to be robbed later that day after I watched YouTube videos of 1600-meter races. I came across one video of a guy in the Olympics running a 3:46 mile. This guy is ranked at the top in the world, and it crushed my confidence. I thought, *Wow, he seriously would've lapped me, and He does my mile pace on his long run.* I caught myself comparing, but I stopped. I reaffirmed how I had prepared well, performed my complete best, and reached my goal.

A study showed that depression is higher in high-income countries versus low to middle-income countries. In fact, approximately fifteen percent were depressed in high-income countries, while eleven percent of the population was depressed in low to middle-income countries.[2] Wonder what the correlation is?

A significantly larger amount of time is spent thinking about meeting basic living requirements in low to middle-income countries, yet they exhibit lower rates of depression. You would think that high-income countries would feel more content, happy, and thankful for the privileges they have.

Or, the more reasonable conclusion is the constant comparison in high-income countries has been a large factor for rising depression levels. High-income countries have more 24/7 access to comparison with social media and have more idle time to let their eyes wander. Priorities become skewed, placing more self-worth in ranks and accomplishments instead of faith, family, and community.

SOCIAL MEDIA PITFALL

Social media has good intentions, but it has some major cons. Some people can scroll through social media without ever comparing or feeling bad about themselves, which is ideal. However, most of us can't resist the urge. We're left with feelings of sadness because we think we don't measure up.

A study published in the journal *JAMA Psychiatry*, revealed that kids who used social media thirty minutes to three hours a day had nearly twice the risk of internalizing mental health problems, compared with kids who didn't use social media at all. The lead researcher Kira Riehm, a doctoral student at Johns Hopkins Bloomberg School of Public Health in Baltimore, concluded that social media's harm on a teen's self-esteem results from the illusion created that everyone else is much happier and better off.

"Even if your life isn't going great, you can make it seem like it's going super well on social media," Riehm said. "It's possible adolescents who are spending a lot of time on social media see people having a great time in their life and doing well, and any issues they have seem much worse."[3] It's easy to forget people are portraying a picture-perfect world, filtering out reality. They're only sharing snippets of their best moments glossed over with their favorite Snapchat filter—it's not real.

DO-YOUR-BEST MINDSET

As a competitive individual, it's hard to resist comparison, especially because I've been playing sports since childhood. Even in academics this last year, being in the top two percent of my class, I initially found myself feeling not good enough. I got my transcript back, and my first thought was, *Aww...If I did X, Y, or Z,*

I could've done better. How ridiculous is that? I thank the Lord for helping me achieve what I did.

The key for me to avoid comparison is first to follow what I feel I'm called to do, and then I must work with a spirit of excellence. If I walk away from something after giving my everything, what good will comparison be when that was all I could do?

When we try to perform good enough to beat someone else, we're limiting ourselves and our full potential.

> WHEN WE TRY TO PERFORM GOOD ENOUGH TO BEAT SOMEONE ELSE, WE'RE LIMITING OURSELVES AND OUR FULL POTENTIAL.

My middle school band director, Mr. Walker, told us before every competition he wouldn't be upset if we got the last place as long as we performed the best we could. Our goal is to reach our potential. This mindset seemed to work because, in three out of our four competitions, we walked away with first place.

When our goal is to perform our best, possibilities are limitless. This mindset takes the pressure off. It also brings the fun back. Keep in mind, we all have our off-days, too. So, if our performance is less than our best, we should be careful not to beat ourselves up over it.

I try to keep this mentality when my mind wants to go into comparison mode, specifically in school or athletics. Instead of questioning where I rank, I ask myself:

Did I prepare as well as I could have?

Did I do everything I could do to become the best version of me?

If I can honestly say yes to these two questions, I don't need a podium to stand on to get the praise of others to feel satisfaction and a sense of accomplishment.

Once at cross country practice, I was amazed to see a larger older woman outside walking with a cane. In the time I ran six miles, she probably went half a mile. But this older woman was so motivating to me. I applaud her for getting out there to improve her health with no concern about how others will view her as they pass. It was a hot day, and she could have made so many excuses to stay home. Instead, she showed up. Who's to say your showing up isn't motivating somebody? You don't have to be the best, but you can inspire someone by simply showing up, doing *your* best, and having a great attitude.

CONTENTMENT

Sometimes, enough will never be enough. If you're waiting to be happy when all your goals are met, and life is perfect, you'll never get there. It's much better to learn to be content in all things.

As a matter of fact, for everyone you wish you were more like, there's as many out there wishing they were more like you.

The happiest people in the world are those who're most grateful. As my dad's corny saying goes, "I have eaty, I have drinky, I have everything I needy."

Comparison was mentioned several times throughout the Bible. It occurred through the story of Rachel and Leah, Joseph and his brothers, and even among Jesus' disciples. 2 Corinthians 10:12 (NIV) says, *"We do not dare to classify or compare ourselves with some who commend themselves. When they measure themselves by themselves and compare themselves with themselves, they are not wise."*

Comparison to others kills each other's dreams and aspirations. Instead of this, we should only compare ourselves to the person we were yesterday. If we all better ourselves, the world around us will be better.

Reinforcements:

- Comparison is the thief of joy.

- A *be the best* expectation is simply unachievable, and it will always leave us never feeling good enough.

- Social media's harm on a teen's self-esteem results from the illusion created that everyone else is much happier and better off.

- When we try to perform good enough to beat someone else, we're limiting our full potential.

- There's no way to be 100% satisfied with yourself and your abilities if you compare yourself to others.

Pause and Ponder:

1. In what areas of your life are you tempted to compare yourself to others?

_____

_____

_____

_____

2. How can you avoid falling into the comparison trap?

_____

_____

_____

_____

13

OVERCOMING SIN

We're all works in progress. We need to embrace the fact we're going to mess up. Mistakes are inevitable. I used to beat myself up every time I goofed, but I'm slowly learning to let the idea of perfection go. We all fall short of God's glory. After all, we're humans, and ever since Adam and Eve ate the forbidden fruit, we live in a fallen world.

However, we can control how we respond when we miss the mark.

Falling short, missing the mark—what am I talking about? Well, I'm not referring to a wrong answer on a math test. I'm talking about disobeying our Heavenly Father.

First, let me back up a minute. Why do we have such a bad connotation of obedience? The beautiful thing about God's love is He doesn't control us like we're a prisoner. It's quite the opposite.

Imagine a train on a train track. It's free to travel all over the country. However, if it ever derails, then we have a big problem. As long as it's on the track, it's fulfilling its purpose.

Likewise, obedience to Jesus Christ illuminates our

> OBEDIENCE TO JESUS CHRIST ILLUMINATES OUR TRUE SELF AND ENABLES US TO FULFILL GOD'S PURPOSE FOR OUR LIVES.

true self and enables us to fulfill God's purpose for our lives. It's when we get off track that we find ourselves spinning our wheels.

Because we're free to choose, out of the hundreds of decisions we make daily, we're bound to make some bad ones, too. But God doesn't want us to get stuck in the mud. The quicker we accept our mistakes, repent, move on, and change, the better. Let's stay on track!

Jesus paid the price on the cross, and through repentance, we can have a fresh start. Repentance is more than remorse for our actions, but it isn't self-condemnation either. We hate the sin, not ourselves.

Famous evangelist, Billy Graham, said, "Hate your false ways, hate your vain thoughts, hate your evil passions, hate your lying, hate your covetousness, hate your greed, but do not hate yourself. Self-hatred leads to self-destruction, and it is wrong to destroy that which was created in God's image."[1]

Repentance is, however, a sincere regret over our sin and a heartfelt desire to walk as Jesus walked in obedience to God.

Sometimes, we must work through the consequences of sin, but no matter what, we can stand forgiven, blameless, and without shame.

How we react to coming up short greatly molds our character. We can either deliberately strive to change and not repeat the same sin in the future, or we can beat ourselves up, feel sorry for ourselves, and miss out on a beautiful and exciting adventure with Christ.

IDOLS

We don't often think of idol worship as being a problem today, but it goes beyond worshipping golden statues. Idols can be anything you set higher than God, such as relationships, good grades, appearances, money, and even church. When prioritized correctly, many of these things are good. But when coveted ahead of God, they quickly become rivals of God. Looking back, I've set many things up in my life as idols without even knowing it. How about you?

We often make the mistake of putting our faith in things that don't matter. Take popularity, for example. Who doesn't want to be well-liked? Social media feeds on this. We've figured out the algorithms to get the most likes and followers, wasting hours of our lives painting a picture-perfect world on all our accounts.

Go to an airport and look at all the people on their phones. Are we focused more on building our platforms than building our relationships with God? Let's start tearing these idols down!

Idols take our focus away from God, and we end up worshipping those things without realizing it. A common idol is money. Again, money on its own isn't bad. But if our pursuit of money is greater than our pursuit of God, we have a problem. Luke 16:13 says, *"No servant can serve two masters, for either he will hate the one and love the other, or he will be devoted to the one and despise the other. You cannot serve God and money."*

STOP DIGGING

So, you've tripped up. Now what? *I've gotten into this, so what's one more time?* This attitude is the pit of our making. A repeated negative action forfeits our chances of winning.

After a mess up, it's easy to feel like we've failed a mission with no retry button. We should be careful to avoid the defeated mindset in which we believe we can't come back after sin. Heaven loves a good comeback story, and I do, too!

I have committed sins repeatedly. Every person has certain sins they struggle with more than others. But I don't accept sin is a part of me or that I'm bound by it. I'm an overcomer by the blood of Jesus and the word of my testimony. The more I resist temptation, the stronger I become in my resolve to overcome.

It's more than a self-promise. I've learned the accountability from others, changing my routine, or hanging around a different group of people helps me overcome.

If you want to get out of that sin, first ask yourself where and why you commit the sin. Is it primarily when you're alone, with a certain group of people, or when in a certain mood? These are simple steps you can take to bypass temptation.

Let's stop digging ourselves further into the pit. It's a death trap, and there's hope. You can change with Jesus Christ because He's the rope to grab hold of to get out of the pit. Put the shovel down and take the rope.

Each day is a new day, so why not today?

WALKING IT OUT

Now that you've grabbed the rope, you've got to pull yourself up and walk it out. It will take courage, discipline, and deliberate goals to break a sinful habit, but you'll feel freer afterward and glad you did it.

For example, maybe your sin is a foul mouth. Challenge yourself to become more aware of your words. Every time you slip and say a bad word, stop, and do five pushups. Over time, you'll become more aware, and you'll start catching yourself before you even say it. Eventually, you'll break this sinful habit, and you'll be building self-discipline and muscle at the same time.

My health teacher told a story about a man who became morbidly obese. He said he worked long shifts on a farm and sat on a tractor for most of the day. The man came home exhausted and spent the rest of the evening sitting in front of the TV, eating large amounts of food.

He knew his lifestyle was unhealthy, but he didn't want to come to terms with how overweight he'd gotten. Therefore, he avoided the scale. He feared seeing the number would make it too real for him.

His wakeup finally came when his doctor told him if he didn't change, he was going to die. It took the fear of death for him to face reality. He sought help, fixed his diet, started exercising, and saw significant progress. After seeing positive results on the scale, hope returned and encouraged him to continue moving in the right direction.

The hardest part of his journey was facing the truth of what he'd become. He was ashamed. But after taking that first step in the right direction, he eventually lost over one-hundred pounds!

Sometimes, that first step is the hardest, and we won't get there overnight. But as we stay disciplined on our journey, we will see results, and it will be well worth it in the end!

POWER OF SHARING

We all have weaknesses and struggles. Opening up to others and asking for help isn't weak. It takes real courage. When we share, it lets us know we aren't alone in the struggle.

Everyone needs someone they feel comfortable talking to who authentically cares for them. That person should make you feel like it's normal to have problems and not something only *bad people* face.

I feel comfortable sharing my problems with my parents. But it could be a friend, grandparent, a youth pastor, or anyone you trust with your best interests in mind. As you've discovered in previous chapters, I've had numerous struggles with addiction and finding balance in life. Others have encouraged me through these struggles.

Sharing also brings your struggle out in the open from a dark hidden place into the light. This alone often loosens the stronghold the struggle had over us. Furthermore, it brings you accountability that lends you the strength to overcome.

RESISTING TEMPTATION

Setting good habits ensures we don't make decisions we'll later regret. Whether that's hanging around with the right group of kids, listening to your parents, or being bold about what you stand for, you'll be less likely to be in hard-to-get-out-of situations.

When you decide for yourself and make it clear to others what you live by, you'll find friends that have similar beliefs as

> SETTING GOOD HABITS
> ENSURES WE DON'T
> MAKE DECISIONS WE'LL
> LATER REGRET.

you. I've been bold about my beliefs, and I've made great friends without even trying.

On the other hand, I've witnessed classmates with wishy-washy personalities easily led by others down the wrong path. They're easily influenced and cave under pressure.

The key here is making up your mind on how you'll stand and what you'll stand for before a tricky situation arises. If you're at a party and offered drugs, you don't even consider it because your mind has already decided, *No, I don't do drugs*.

Don't put yourself in compromising situations. Be bold from the beginning and refuse to bow to the will of others. Let your *no* be mighty and your *yes* committed.

FORGIVENESS

We all fall short, but there's a perfect One. Thankfully, we can find forgiveness through the sacrifice of Jesus Christ. He endured the cross, laying down His life, so we're cleansed of all our sins.

Sin may feel good but leaves us with regret afterward. Sin is a false sense of fulfillment. Sin separates us from our Father.

Through Jesus, we have restored relationship with God. We trade our filthy garments, and He places a robe of righteousness upon our shoulders. Not because we earned it, but because He loves us so much. He died for us so we could be with Him.

Redemption is free. We must only ask. God is always there with open arms, waiting patiently, and He's so happy when we come back to Him.

Reinforcement

- Obedience to Jesus Christ illuminates our true self and enables us to fulfill God's purpose for our lives.

- Idols can be anything we set higher than God.

- The more we resist temptation, the stronger we become in our resolve to overcome.

- It'll take courage, discipline, and deliberate goals to break a sinful habit, but you'll feel freer afterwards and glad you did it.

- Sharing brings our struggles out in the open, loosens the stronghold, and brings the accountability that lends you the strength to overcome.

- Don't put yourself in compromising situations.

- Through Jesus, we can have forgiveness for our sins.

Pause and Ponder:

1. In what ways are you coming up short? Ask God to expose any sin in your life you need to repent of.

_____

_____

_____

_____

2. What are some simple strategies you can use to avoid finding yourself in compromising situations?

_____

_____

_____

_____

14

FINDING GODLY INFLUENCES

W e shouldn't allow merely anyone to speak into our life. We need to choose our friends and mentors wisely. Chaplain Ronnie Melancon said, "Show me your friends and I'll show you your future."[1] Yes, it's that important. Good influencers can help you envision things you never thought possible. They're loyal when life gets hard. They push you when you're ready to give up. Essentially, a good, Godly influencer will make you a better person.

These people are rare finds. If you have a person like this in your life, treasure them. If not, pray God sends someone your way.

So, does this mean we should ditch everyone else? No way. We're to be a friend to all, but not everyone gets our back-stage passes. It's super wise for us to set different access levels. Boundaries are healthy.

I like to think of it as the temple of God. In the Old Testament, the temple had an outer court, an inner court, and the Holy of Holies. The temple is a great picture of the access we give people in our lives.

We have acquaintances in the outer court. These are our small talk friends. "Hi, how are you doing?" Everything stays on the surface. Then, we have those who we allow into the inner court.

This group can be known as our inner circle. We usually have a lot in common with these people. They're our buddies, teammates, and the ones we call to hangout. We share our dreams and aspirations and crushes with our inner court circle, but not necessarily our fears, hurts, and temptations.

In the Old Testament, the Holy of Holies is where the presence of God dwelled. Only the priest was allowed entrance here and only once a year at that. Similarly, and forgive me if this sounds weird, but only a select few are allowed into your Holy of Holies. These people have earned a place into your heart and proven themselves trustworthy. They have your best interests in mind. To these noble people, you can share all—the good, the bad, and the ugly—and their love for you won't change. They'll keep you accountable when life gets tough.

The boundaries are fluid like cell membranes, meaning people may come and go between the inner and outer courts. A famous quote attributed to Michelle Ventor says, "People come into your life for a reason, a season, or a lifetime."[2] Some will come into your life to use you or because they want something from you. Others, you may get along with for a short time then split ways. Then, there are those rare finds who'll stick with us for a lifetime. We need to recognize and differentiate who belongs where. And for those only around for a season, may we treasure the time we had together and be mature enough to let go.

WHO'S IN YOUR COURT?

We all need friends, but the friends we choose are a big deal. I'm sure you've heard of the phrase, "You're known by the company you keep." Proverbs 13:20 puts it this way. *He who walks with wise men will be wise, but the companion of fools will suffer harm.*

Many teens think they have friends but don't. Real friends build us up, not tear us down. Around them, we should be comfortable to get real without fearing they'll use it against us or tell others. We shouldn't have to act like someone we're not to appease them. Real friends make us want to be a better version of our self, and they don't lead us into making decisions we'll regret afterward. Now ask yourself, are the ones you're hanging around real friends?

Habeeb Akande, a British-born writer and historian, said, "Fake friends are like shadows: always near you at your brightest moments, but nowhere to be seen at your darkest hour. True friends are like stars, you don't always see them, but they are always there."[3]

Fake friends will only be around when you're popular, successful, and wealthy but will immediately leave you when these things disappear. They're only there to use you for their sake. They have their interests in mind, not yours, and they'll disappear as soon as problems arise. The truth of the matter is, they don't truly care about you as an individual. It's best to keep our distance with these people.

Oprah Winfrey has had her fair share of fake friend experiences. She says, "Lots of people want to ride with you in the limo, but what you want is someone who'll take the bus with you when the limo breaks down."[4]

> "LOTS OF PEOPLE WANT TO RIDE WITH YOU IN THE LIMO, BUT WHAT YOU WANT IS SOMEONE WHO'LL TAKE THE BUS WITH YOU WHEN THE LIMO BREAKS DOWN."[4]

It's primarily the people with a lot to offer who need to be mindful of who's present in their court. It's wise to ask God for discernment so we can see people's true intentions. In doing so, we'll save ourselves a lot of anguish and hurt.

AVOID THE DEBBIE-DOWNERS

The things others say and speak into our lives matter because it takes many positive comments to build someone up, but only one or two negative comments can tear someone down. Unfortunately, it seems we listen more to the negativity.

Negativity sticks like Velcro, while positivity sticks more like a Post-it Note. It's hard in practice, but we need to yank off the

Velcro, so the negativity won't stick. And we need to hammer in the Post-it Notes.

It's exhausting to hang around with a negative person who complains. The woe-is-me attitude is highly contagious, and you can quickly start taking on these traits as well until everything becomes gloom and doom.

Complaining and throwing pity-parties never helps a situation. Conservative political commentator Ben Shapiro said, "I've never seen anyone's life get better by complaining about reality. I've seen it get better by accepting reality as it is and then making personal decisions to make it better."[5] Life gets tough for all of us. I used to complain often, but when I discovered complaining only wastes time and makes the situation seem worse, I decreased my number of complaints.

Almost every highly accomplished person has been discouraged by others. To get past this, they must do one of two things. They must discern the negative from the positive comments and let the negative go in one ear and out the other. Or, they can view the negativity as fuel to drive them even harder, proving their naysayers wrong with a private response of, *we'll see about that.*

GO AGAINST THE FLOW

We must believe strongly in ourselves because scrutiny will come from every direction. Even family members can look at what we're doing and tell us to do something more reasonable or less risky. You won't do anything spectacular if you follow in the same footsteps of everyone else. Follow the footsteps of Christ.

We need to avoid hanging around the wrong crowd because they can turn us into an entirely different person. Let's face it. As a teenager, we're impressionable. The surrounding crowd can heavily influence good kids. It's important to discover your crowd, but usually, it's best to go against the flow. 1 Corinthians 15:33 says, *"Do not be deceived: Bad company ruins good morals."* It's easier to make bad decisions when those around you are also making bad decisions.

Thankfully, I've been blessed to have great friends. Most of them do cross country with me. I feel we have a healthy balance between joking around, having a good time, and knowing when to be serious. Each person has something to offer to the conversation. We work daily to better each other in cross country running and as individuals. They inspire me to be a better person. They all are genuine, hardworking, disciplined, humorous, and personable.

But I wouldn't necessarily say these kids are the most popular in the school. Sure, they're all very well-liked. But our definition of cool is slightly different than the majority of kids in my school. We value work ethic, academics, God, and family. Most kids my age value social status, appearances, and themselves.

Sadly, the immoral culture we live in is quick to take us in a direction away from what God has for us. Our culture encourages us to compromise our values. But we don't have to give in to the wickedness around us. We refuse to say, "If you can't beat 'em, join 'em." No, instead we know, as James 4:4 says, *"Whoever wishes to be a friend of the world makes himself an enemy of God."* We're in the world, but not of it.

FIND THOSE WHO INSPIRE YOU

Try surrounding yourself with optimists. Optimists inspire you to pursue dreams so big they instill fear within you. Pessimists will destroy these dreams making them seem too far-fetched, too unlikely, and impossible. Without taking some chances, we may never achieve our dreams.

I challenge you and your friends to a little activity. This is great for youth groups, too. Sometime, while you're hanging out, write down at least one uplifting comment about each person in your circle. Maybe you've thought it, but never verbalized it. I could say something positive about everyone I know, but sadly, I don't tell them enough. I want to get better at that.

Many members of my church met at an older couple's house for a mini-service one Wednesday night. At the end of the message, we listed positive comments about each person for a minute or two. It was a practice in how we see others through the eyes of Christ.

The words they shared that night truly spoke to me, and I cling to every one of them. I keep this list and refer to when I feel down or when the enemy is feeding me lies about myself. This list reminds me of who I am in Christ and the potential and purpose He's given me. These are words of life to me!

Going to this meeting with prophetic adults has hugely impacted my life, and my turn was probably a total of only two minutes. It goes to show how quickly we can change a life. Our words matter. Proverbs 18:21 says, *"Death and life are in the power of the tongue, and those who love it will eat its fruits."*

Other's opinions mean nothing unless it's out of love and from God. Teens need to know we should listen to the voice filled with love and not hate and bitterness. The wisdom of Godly influences will cut through the darkness and shed light on situations. They'll illuminate solutions you hadn't seen before. Glean from their wisdom. Hold fast to their counsel.

BE TEACHABLE

Jordan Peterson, a renowned clinical psychologist and Professor at the University of Toronto, wrote a bestselling book, *12 Rules for Life*. One rule stood out to me. It reads, "Assume that the person you are listening to might know something you don't."[6]

> WHEN WE LISTEN TO OTHERS' LIFE STORIES, WE WALK AWAY WITH VALUABLE LIFE LESSONS.

We can gain knowledge by our willingness to listen to people older than us. Everyone comes from a different background with different experiences. When we listen to others' life stories, we walk away with valuable life lessons.

Likewise, the smartest man alive can no doubt learn something from you and me. None of us have all the answers, but all of us have some of the answers. Until we learn to be open in our understanding, we'll only see the world from our vantage point.

We'll miss the beauty and wisdom in others' views and perspectives. We'll have false confidence regarding our beliefs when we keep only our view of situations.

When you believe in something strongly like your faith, it's still okay to hear others' reasonings for their beliefs. When you gather all the information, you can separate facts from false evidence. In the end, your truth becomes much stronger because it's more validated. Then, you're able to make educated and passionate arguments of your beliefs. Know why you believe what you do, and you'll become unshakable.

Proverbs 19:20 (ESV) says, *"Listen to advice and accept instruction, that you may gain wisdom in the future."* I hope the people you're allowing to influence you are Godly people who offer wise counsel. The Bible should be our plumb line. If their counsel lines up with the word, the chances are good that it's wisdom speaking.

FIND A SPOTTER

Anyone who lifts weights needs a spotter to help them when lifting more than what they're accustomed to. The strongest professional weightlifters have as many as three huge men around them for their protection. We all need spotters in our life.

When things become too hard and heavy for us to bear, we need Godly influences to help us. God didn't intend for us to walk this journey alone. Like serious injuries can occur when weightlifters don't have a spot to help them when their strength gives way, we can make bad decisions and find ourselves in a deep pit if we don't have enough guidance. And even then, we still may fall, but it's incredibly wise to have those trusted friends and mentors around to help pull you out of the pit.

As I've heard pastor Bill Johnson say, "If you want to go fast, go alone. If you want to go far, go with others."

Reinforcements:

- You're known by the company you keep.

- Fake friends will only be around when you're popular, successful, and wealthy but will immediately leave you when these things disappear.

- Hanging around someone filled with complaining and negativity can derail you.

- Bad company ruins good morals.

- Find people who inspire you and make you better.

- None of us have all the answers, but all of us have some of the answers.

- We're to be a friend to all, but not everyone gets our backstage passes.

Pause and Ponder:

1. Who's in your court? Using the circles below, fill in those who're in your inner circle (intimate confidants), those who're in your middle circle (friends), and those who're in your outer circle (acquaintances).

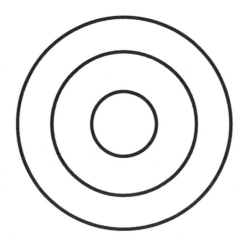

2. Is there anyone you're giving access to the inner circle that needs to move to another ring?

_____

_____

_____

_____

PART 3:

LAND

This is Your Captain Speaking:
Fasten Your Seatbelts and Prepare for Landing

The landing pad is in sight. You've learned the disciplines of priority setting, time management, minimizing stress, resting properly, handling addiction, dodging comparison, and finding Godly influences. In no time, you'll be living out these successful habits and fulfilling your unique purpose. Now it's time to stay the course. Your God-appointed destiny is ahead.

15

LEAVING YOUR IMPRINT

Tragically, people are becoming more isolated now than in previous years. According to a 2018 national survey by Cigna, loneliness levels have reached an all-time high, with nearly half of surveyors reporting they sometimes or always feel alone.[1]

Electronics are a significant factor contributing to the suffering of personal interaction. Instantly, we can text our friends, tune in to a weather forecast, download a song, order groceries, and stream a movie online—all from the comforts of our own home. Why do we need to interact with the world in person when we can easily do it from our fingertips?

I'm not sure what your school policy is on electronics, but in my school, whenever we have down-time in class, most people go straight to their phone, never saying a word to the people around them. We've lost the art of communication. In doing so, we're shaped more by social media rather than real-life people. And perhaps even sadder, unless you've reached influencer status, what kind of impact are you making in the world around you?

God put us on this earth to interact with others. The world needs you. You have special gifts and a unique personality to share with others. We're all called to love the person in front of us and make them feel like they matter. Burying our head in our phones doesn't exactly give off a *we care about you* message.

I understand some are better at being social and talking with people than others. But social interaction is one of several ways we can impact others. You don't have to be a brilliant communicator to look someone in the eyes and offer a smile as you pass them in the hall. That simple act tells them you've seen and acknowledged them. People want that.

MARKS OF A GOOD LEADER

First, let me clarify what I mean by impacting others. By impacting others, I don't mean to try to change someone. You can only influence others; you can't directly change them. Everyone decides for themselves if they change and in what way.

> YOU CAN ONLY INFLUENCE OTHERS; YOU CAN'T DIRECTLY CHANGE THEM.

Even with good intentions, forcefully trying to change someone else comes off as thinking you're better than them. People like to do things for themselves and want to have the freedom to decide how they want to live.

For example, you wouldn't want to walk in a store and have someone pressure you to buy something, even if you came in for that product. This turns people off. We like making decisions from our own will. Right? We like to choose from options rather than having something pushed down our throats. We'll refuse to swallow it for spite, even if it might taste good. Blame it on the hormones because teens especially like to be a little rebellious.

Do you know what a good leader does? First, they take ownership of the problem. Then, a good leader will come into the problematic situation with a solution already in mind. But rather than informing others of the resolution, they'll present questions, possibilities, and scenarios that will lead the group of those involved to come up with the same solution they already had in mind. Everyone walked away feeling like they contributed to the answer. People who're involved in solving the problem are much more likely to follow through. They exert greater effort to make the solution a success.

A good leader is okay not being the hero. They're not afraid to give power to the people because they're guiding and impacting decision making. Notice, I said guiding and impacting—not manipulating. There's a huge difference here. Manipulators say, "If you scratch my back, I'll scratch yours." They give but are always looking for something back in return. Beware of these people—they can't be trusted.

SOMEONE IS ALWAYS WATCHING

As creepy as it sounds, there's always someone viewing how you act and respond to situations around you. Like it or not, everyone you encounter walks away with an opinion of you. What impression are you leaving with them?

We need to reflect Christ in all we do. People are attracted to those with a positive outlook on life and with a loving personality. In a world that drains the life out of you, these guys and gals are a breath of fresh air.

It's so important to be genuine. We can talk the talk, but we must back it up with our walk, or we're hypocritical. Inky Johnson made an impactful quote, "Some people don't need you to preach them a sermon but live one."[2] It's much easier to preach to others about doing something than actually doing it yourself. However, positively impacting others by living it out loud is stronger than telling them how to live. Much of what I write are things I struggle with the same as you. I'm not going to lie about it and say I've got it all together. We're all imperfect, so why not be honest about it as we strive to improve together?

Have any of you with younger siblings ever heard your parents say, *They really look up to you?* I've seen evidence of impacting others from my brother, Elijah. He's five-and-a-half years younger than me, yet he acts so much older than he really is. I guess I'll take the credit for that. Because we're around each other so often, he imitates some of the things I do. He acts much older than his actual age because of my unintentional impact on him. I didn't grow up nearly as fast as he has because I have no older sibling. I'm sure those of you with brothers and sisters can relate.

We have a poster of Albert Einstein in my geometry classroom with a quote that says, "Setting an example isn't the main means of influencing others, it's the only means."[3] Various evidence proves that humans learn by watching others.

University of Michigan psychologist Robert Zajonc conducted an experiment. He decided to take pictures of newlywed couples and another photo of the couple twenty-five years after marriage. Every couple had a similar result.

The man and woman's appearances became more alike in the second photograph. The happier the couple claimed their marriage was, the closer in resemblance they became. Zajonc concluded that individuals begin mimicking the people they're around the most. The couples, therefore, produced similar facial expressions.[4]

The forty-three facial muscles work the same as any other muscle. The more often a particular muscle is used, the more it's accentuated. Certain muscles in the face will be used more, depending on the frequency of facial expressions, subsequently becoming more visible. As a result, if a couple smiles often, they'll most likely have higher cheekbones by using those facial muscles more than a couple who smiles less.

So, the married couples developed similar expression muscles as the years went on. What kind of expressions are you helping those around you develop?

You see, we're all given a sphere of influence. You can leave a positive imprint or a negative one. Some people bring joy everywhere they go, while some bring joy when they go.

SOME PEOPLE BRING JOY EVERYWHERE THEY GO, WHILE SOME BRING JOY WHEN THEY GO.

What if we made it our intention to positively impact our sphere of influence, making their righteousness, discipline, honor system, and joyful expressions more evident in their actions?

And then they, in turn, impacted their spheres of influence similarly? Talk about a ripple effect! This would change our whole culture.

Let's learn to live a life reflecting God and His kingdom principles so we can effectively and positively impact the world around us.

SMALL THINGS ARE WHAT COUNTS

Often, we think we have to do something extravagant to make someone's day, but really, it's our small actions that leave the biggest imprint. Whether it's a simple hello or a smile, it means more to the other person than you think. And let's face it—we like to hang around those who make us feel good.

One super-easy way we can positively impact others is by giving sincere compliments. Say it like you mean it. You can be sure when we say something to validate someone, not only will you have made them feel significant, but they'll likely not forget it anytime soon. And literally, it may take five seconds of your day, but the life you've put back into their day is significant.

It's easy to approach someone and say with a smile, "Hey, how's your day going?" Again, say it like you mean it and really care. Don't overcomplicate the simple things. We may consider sharing a compliment with someone, then hesitate. After hesitation, we likely talk ourselves out of it and say nothing.

We may fear the opposite sex will misinterpret our intentions, think we're weird, or see more into it than we intend. We need to get over ourselves and our insecurities. When we've created a society where it's weird to be nice, then we've got issues. Let's change it!

Compliments and encouragement are priceless. Simply loving people spurs them to grow and flourish. Love births hope, and with hope, the possibilities are endless. If we withhold this because we're afraid of what others will think, then we're selfish.

Furthermore, we don't need to limit compliments to only those who're kind to us. The people who aren't kind need encouragement the most, and you could be the only one to provide it. They may not immediately express gratitude, but we should never underestimate the impact we've had on them.

To this day, I still remember the compliment my freshman biology teacher said to me as I was leaving class. He said something like, "You really seem like a good kid, Noah. I appreciate you for that." Those four seconds made me feel great, and three years later, I still remember it. He had my respect before, but because he honored me, he instantly gained my honor toward him. Likewise, I want to create a culture of honor.

BEAR ONE ANOTHER'S BURDENS

When we make it our intention to honor others, we make ourselves more approachable. Earlier, I said people like to hang around those who make them feel good. When this becomes our lifestyle, we'll start noticing people will come to us when they're struggling because they know we'll make them feel better. They'll start to trust us, knowing we mean it when we say, *How's it going?*

This gives you a great opportunity to offer to pray for them. While you may not have the solution to their problem, you know the One who does. Galatians 6:2 tells us, *"Bear one another's burdens."*

Everyone needs someone they can talk to who's a good influence in their life. You could be the only person to offer that precious gift to them. And again, it's the simplicity that counts. May we never underestimate the influence a listening ear offers. You may not give any ground-breaking advice, but by listening, you've lifted a burden off their shoulders.

FROM CHRIST'S PERSPECTIVE

What if we viewed others how God views them? God doesn't treat people differently based on popularity, physical appearance, or how much they can offer Him. Whether it's a six-foot-tall captain of the football team or a scrawny kid who gets bullied, He loves them both equally. Whereas, we tend to either be intimidated by the football player or poke fun of the scrawny kid. This shouldn't be.

My parents have told me no matter who someone is, they still put their pants on the same way as everyone else. The football player acts tough on the outside, but it doesn't mean he's tough internally. He probably needs someone who won't bow to him because of his popularity but someone who he can be real around without fear of judgment. He might conform to how others want him to act, when in reality, he wants love from people who care about him as a person.

What about the scrawny kid? Maybe he isn't a talented athlete because he has always had his nose buried in a book. This kid probably has a brilliant mind but is intimidated to share it. So, instead, he remains quiet and closed-off, hoping to go unnoticed.

Bullies are like a crab, who display a hard-outer shell, but really have hidden sensitivities. Shells protect or shield outsiders from seeing the vulnerability inside. So, usually, those who act crabby have a sensitivity they don't want others to see. But God sees through the tough-guy shield. He knows the struggles and the hurts, and He longs to heal those areas.

God wants the football player to live authentically and to use his popularity to influence others positively. And God wants the scrawny kid to be comfortable in his skin and own who God created him to be.

Everyone is imperfect and has insecurities. But at the same time, we all have unique gifts and talents to offer. Let's try to see others from Christ's perspective. Then, we can pull out the gold in them rather than focusing on the dirt.

RIGHTING WRONGS

Obviously, our goal is to leave a positive imprint on others. But what happens when we've negatively affected someone else? Let's admit it. The teenagers' mood is like a roller coaster. We can be in a good mood for one minute and a bad mood the next. We blame it on the hormones. But what if we took one of our lousy mood moments out on someone?

While it's best to be silent during these moments, sometimes our emotions get the best of us. It's when we're in a bad mood our character is tested the most. Anyone can be a light to others when things are going well, but few can continue to be a light when things aren't going well. It's in these moments we need to learn how to conduct ourselves.

As soon as we realize we've wronged someone, we need to go to that person and apologize. It's now up to them to forgive you. We can't undo our wrongs, but God can restore anything, whether it's relationships, time, or lost opportunities. The Israelites in the Old Testament had a whole harvest destroyed through the swarms of locusts. God promises the impossible in Joel 2:25 (NKJV) saying, *"I will restore to you the years that the swarming locust has eaten."* God always follows through with his promises. Their fields yielded an abundance that made up for what was lost.[5]

The main people we impact are our friends. We need to treat them well, remain loyal, and have their best interests in mind. We need to rejoice when they rejoice and be sad when they're sad. And we need not let the sun go down before we've asked their forgiveness for a harsh word. This is how you earn a friend and keep a friend.

THE RIPPLE EFFECT

When we think of leaving an imprint on others, we get excited. We think big and are ready to change the world. However good our intentions are, this shouldn't be our focus. Allow me to share a quick account from a Monk written approximately 1100 AD. It's still relevant today.

When I was a young man, I wanted to change the world.

I found it was difficult to change the world, so I tried to change my nation.

When I found I couldn't change the nation, I began to focus on my town.

I couldn't change the town and as an older man, I tried to change my family.

Now, as an old man, I realize the only thing I can change is myself, and suddenly I realize that if long ago, had changed myself, I could have made an impact on my family.

My family and I could have made an impact on our town.

Their impact could have changed the nation and I could indeed have changed the world.[6]

Your influence spreads whether you want it to or not. Remember, you're the light. Lighting someone else's candle doesn't make yours darker. It makes the room brighter.

Reinforcements:

- We're all called to love the person in front of us and make them feel like they matter.

- Good leaders take ownership of problems, and they're okay with not being the hero, sharing power with the people.

- Positively impacting others by living it out loud is stronger than telling them how to live.

- It's often the unkind people who need encouragement the most, and you could be the only one to provide it.

- Instead of trying to change the world, change yourself. Then, the ripple effect will naturally happen.

Pause and Ponder:

1. How are you positively impacting your sphere of influence?

_____

_____

_____

_____

2. How can you improve your leadership skills?

_____

_____

_____

_____

3. In what ways would you like to see the world change? How are your actions making a difference?

_____

_____

_____

_____

16

FULFILLING YOUR DREAMS

Most everyone has dreams, goals, and aspirations. The question to ask ourselves is, *What are we doing today that will help us activate these aspirations, achieve these goals, and fulfill these dreams?*

The Law of Diminishing Intent states the longer you wait to do something you should do now, the greater the odds are you'll never actually do it.[1] When the moment of inspiration hits, we should take action. The longer we sit on it, the less motivated we'll be to do it. Immediately start planning the necessary work to reach your goals and then take small, consistent action towards them.

Even if you're sixteen years old and your dream is to own a business someday, you can still do something about it today. With no degree and no money, you may wonder how. One good idea is to read as many leadership and business savvy books you can get your hands on. This is valuable information that will ensure success when the day comes for you to open your business.

When it comes to fulfilling your dreams, we often think we need to wait for the right moment. Truly, if you try waiting for the right time, it may not come. But the dream will come to fruition with the right connections, some perseverance, and a whole lot of grit.

MAKING SACRIFICES

Your dream won't happen only because you want it to. You must sacrifice for it. There's no shortcut or secret to success other than putting the work in then giving it time to work.

Our cross-country races are on Saturdays in the fall, and most of the school football games are on Friday night. I wanted to go to the football games and have fun with friends, but I couldn't do it at the expense of my performance the next day. I knew if I went, I'd eat junk and not get proper sleep.

While the world is having fun, we need to be okay with working hard for our dreams. Galatians 6:9 tells us, *"Let us not lose heart in doing good, for in due time we will reap if we do not grow weary."* One day, our hard work will pay off. As the old saying goes, "If you don't sacrifice for what you want, what you want will become the sacrifice."[2]

Take the farmer, for example. His work requires a significant amount of time, preparation, and dedication to produce rich crops to harvest months later. He must tend the crops every day, and he won't see the fruit of his labor for many months. What we see in the market didn't get there overnight. Likewise, your success won't be overnight, either.

INPUT = OUTPUT

Grades are one of my top priorities. Since I don't have much time outside of school, I have to work on my homework during school downtime, or I won't get it done.

I have a class every day called Studio, another word for study hall. Last year, it was a thirty-minute free class for advanced placement (honor) students. I, along with about three others, worked on homework during this time. I could have been on my phone like the other twenty-seven students, wasting my time, complaining about why I'm not doing well in school, and blaming it on everyone but myself. But instead, I chose grind over laziness.

It requires discipline to do the work when we don't want to do it. I was tempted to watch YouTube videos on my phone and relax. But the payoff was worth it. I have good grades because I do what I have to do to earn them.

Very few things in this world are free. Don't go through life expecting handouts. You'll appreciate things

> YOU'LL APPRECIATE THINGS YOU EARN MUCH MORE THAN THINGS THAT ARE GIVEN TO YOU.

you earn much more than things that are given to you.

STRIVE FOR EXCELLENCE, NOT PERFECTION

When it comes to setting and reaching your goals, never sell yourself short or take shortcuts or be short-sighted. You're more capable than you realize. There's no quick detours to success. Shortcuts only rob you of the valuable knowledge you gain along the way. And always think long-term. As the expression goes, we overestimate what we can accomplish in one year and underestimate what we can accomplish in five years.

Strive for excellence in everything you do—not perfection. There's a difference. Striving for excellence means doing the best we can. Perfectionism is how it sounds, attempting to do something and expecting it to turn out perfectly. Excellence acknowledges effort. Perfectionism acknowledges performance.

I've been a perfectionist at times, and I encourage other teens to avoid this trap. No matter how good I was, I still beat myself up for the smallest flaw. I was always unsatisfied after doing anything because I believed I should've and could've done better. Nothing ever is completely perfect.

On the flipside, *settling* or *good enough* is as bad as perfectionism. In our world today, few people strive to achieve excellence but accept mediocrity instead. Most people choose entertainment over learning and self-development. We spend a lot of time in our cars. Think about how much we'd learn if we listened to educational audiobooks or podcasts over the music blaring through the radio. A spirit of excellence wastes nothing and gives everything.

Speaking to Navy SEAL graduates, David Goggins, a once three-hundred-pound man who, through extreme discipline, became a Navy SEAL, said, "We live in a world where mediocrity is often rewarded. These men up here detest mediocrity." David's story is unbelievable. He lost one-hundred six pounds in three months and completed "Hell Week" on his third and final attempt finally achieving this great honor.[3]

Only a few of the many participants complete Hell Week without ringing the bell. When a soldier rings the bell, it allows them to quit because they can't take it any longer. The more bell rings the remaining soldiers hear, the more tempting it is to join them and be like everyone else. The men who pushed through to complete the training were operating with excellence. It required everything they had, but they didn't cave. Becoming a Navy SEAL is one of the most prestigious ranks of honor, requiring exceptional performance and discipline.

When you're doing push-ups and start feeling the pain, the mediocrity can stop if you push past the discomfort. When you think you can't do one more, then do five more. Keep pushing when things get hard. This is how you make progress and see improvement. Reaching your dreams won't be an easy task. Don't let obstacles get in the way.

Remove the word *quit* from your vocabulary. I'm sure some of the men who rang that bell later asked themselves, "What if I had gone a little more? What if I had hung in there a little further? Was that really all the pain I could take?"

If you want to be extraordinary, you must be willing to do what the ordinary won't.

POSITION FOR SUCCESS

Hard work doesn't guarantee success. You may experience rejection and failure along the way. Most don't realize being willing to fail puts you in the best position to be successful.

Blogger, Anthony Moore, wrote, "The most important goals you have should be experiential learning and personal transformation. If you're always chasing success, it will constantly elude you. But if you always prioritize incredible personal transformation and paradigm-shifting experiences, success will gravitate towards you as if you were a magnet."[4]

My coach's goal for our team at the beginning of last year's cross-country season was not to win state. It was to be *in a position* to win state. Anything could happen on the day of the event. The projected winner could have a great day with five runners under sixteen minutes for a 5K race, and there's no way we could win. However, even the best have bad days. We want to be able to take advantage of the situation if the top couple of schools had an off-day to give us a chance at winning.

On race day, our team had pretty good times, but the top two schools had even better times. We ended up taking third place, and we were happy with that. Considering we're a public school and the other two teams recruit because they're both private schools, I'd say we did really well.

Joshua Bell, one of the nation's best violinists, took part in a social experiment by playing his 3.5 million-dollar violin in the D.C. metro subway station two days after a sold-out theatre in Boston, with tickets averaging one-hundred dollars. He played the same music but dressed like a beggar and sat out a pot for donations.

Only seven out of the few thousand passers-by stopped to listen to his music in the forty-five minutes he played. That's about one in every 429 people! Only one person recognized him as the famous violinist, and he received no money for his performance.[5]

If you're rejected or ignored by others, it doesn't mean you aren't qualified or good at what you do. Sometimes, you can be rejected regardless of skill because of your lack of qualifications, connections, platform, or tools.

In this social experiment, Bell didn't position himself for success. He had all the talent in the world but didn't surround himself with people that would appreciate his gift. Therefore, his talent was shunned.

If you've the passion and the talent for something, study the best of your field of interest. Discover what they did to get to where they are today. If at all possible, friend them. Write them a note explaining how much you look up to them and describe how they've influenced you for the better. Maybe they'll take you under their wing and mentor you.

Never underestimate the power of connection. Continually surround yourself with people who're more successful and smarter than you. You'll be surprised at how much you'll glean from them.

BE PRACTICAL

When it comes to achieving your goals, the more practical they are, the more likely you are to stick to them. For example, if your end game is huge, set up smaller, more attainable goals so you can better track your progress.

At age thirteen, I wanted the latest iPhone. My parents said they'd pay half if I'd pay the rest. I didn't have the money, so this incentivized me to start my first business. That summer, I decided I was going to do something I enjoyed and earn some money. At the time, I lived on a golf course, so my entrepreneur-self decided I was going into the golf ball selling business.

During early evening hours, I started collecting lost balls from around the lake, surrounding woods, and tall grass around the golf course. I found tons of balls, brought them home, and cleaned them up. After a good scrub, they looked almost brand new. I set up a makeshift shop next to a couple of the holes where golfers had to pass me. I had my hand-made sign with a menu of my selection and their respective pricing. I charged more for the Pro-V's than the Pinnacle's, but it was still a third less than if the golfer bought them brand new.

In the end, all the work paid off, and I had fun doing it as well. My only investment was ten dollars on a good golf ball fetcher. That summer, I ended up collecting probably a few hundred golf balls and made almost five-hundred dollars. It was a win-win for both the golfers and me. The golfers were getting quality balls at about seventy percent off store price, and I got that phone I wanted.

DON'T PUT ALL YOUR EGGS IN ONE BASKET

Investing in many things is good, especially during our teen years, because we have the potential to accomplish many things. The teen years are a time when we haven't necessarily zoned in on *the one thing*. It's good to be involved in a variety of things to keep you busy and to help you find out what you like to do the most.

If you're only doing one thing, you might experience burn out, or you may start to lose interest. Being well-rounded is good. It will expose you to more people with different skill sets and more opportunities. It'll also give you a more complex understanding of yourself—what you like and dislike.

These are the years to expand our horizons. Join a new club. Learn another instrument. Taste something you've never eaten before. Volunteer in your community. Go on a mission trip. Be adventurous, bold, and daring. There's a whole world out there waiting for you to discover it.

REFLECT YOUR BELIEFS

If you believe in something, your actions should reflect it. Say you dream of a cleaner earth with less waste. You should be involved in organizations with this same mission and purposefully involve yourself to shrink your carbon footprint. Be the change you want to see.

I found a funny meme with a famous actor who, when asked by the media about climate change, replied, "It's scary to know it's been proven through science that climate change is due to human activity, and we continue to ignore it. The only voice we really have is through voting."[6] Then, it showed a headline of their twenty-five-million-dollar private jet making an emergency landing because of an engine failure.

Don't get me wrong, I love this person's acting, but if they truly believed in climate change, they wouldn't own a private jet for travel. I wouldn't say I like to make assumptions about others, but based on my research, it's safe to say that this person's carbon footprint is much larger than the average person.

Backing beliefs up with action is the making of a good leader. People will respect you because you're committed to the cause, but they'll follow you because you're leading by example. ... Put your money where your mouth is.

> PEOPLE WILL RESPECT YOU BECAUSE YOU'RE COMMITTED TO THE CAUSE, BUT THEY'LL FOLLOW YOU BECAUSE YOU'RE LEADING BY EXAMPLE.

THE GRAVEYARD

Countless people have had great ideas and excellent dreams but lacked the follow-through to see them realized. American author, Les Brown, said, "The graveyard is the richest place on earth, because it's here that you will find all the hopes and dreams that were never fulfilled, the books that were never written, the songs that were never sung, the inventions that were never shared, the cures that were never discovered, all because someone was too afraid to take that first step."[7]

What if there was a genius who was one attempt away at developing a superfood to combat world hunger? What if there was someone on the brink of curing cancer but couldn't get access to proper research facilities? What if the bank rejected a small business loan needed to create the most fuel-efficient, affordable car?

What if they gave up because of these obstacles and setbacks and never fulfilled those dreams? Throughout history, inventions seem crazy to the average mind until physically in use. I'm sure fifty years ago, the thought of a mobile phone that would serve as a theater, a library, a radio station, a map, and a camera all rolled up into a portable communication device would've been absolutely absurd.

What's holding you back from fulfilling your hopes and dreams? The fullest life is the one poured out. Don't take your unfulfilled purpose to the grave with you.

Reinforcements:

- There's no shortcut or secret to success other than putting the work in, and then giving it time to work.

- It requires discipline to do the work when we don't want to do it.

- Strive for excellence, not perfectionism. And never settle for mediocrity.

- If you want to be extraordinary, you must be willing to do what the ordinary won't.

- People will respect you because you're committed to the cause, but they'll follow you because you're leading by example.

- If you want something or believe in something, talk with your actions.

- Strive to put yourself in a position for success and avoid being intimidated by the possibility of failure.

Pause and Ponder:

1. Do you struggle with perfectionism or settling for mediocrity? If so, how has this limited you?

_____

_____

———————————————————————

———————————————————————

2. How can you better position yourself for success?

———————————————————————

———————————————————————

———————————————————————

———————————————————————

17

FACING FAILURE

Most highly accomplished people don't view failure as a negative thing. They understand success won't occur overnight, and bumps in the road don't stop them. When they fail, they recover quickly and learn from their mistakes.

It's crucial to maintain our confidence in life. Instead of getting down and out when we mess up, we should take a different approach. Often, we fail forward into progress. Through trial and error, eventually we learn what works.

Here's a little warning. The enemy will lie to us and say that because we failed, then we're a failure.

The word tells us in Psalm 37:23-24 (NLT), *"The Lord directs the steps of the godly. He delights in every detail of their lives. Though they stumble, they will never fall, for the Lord holds them by the hand."*

We can't allow failure to have the last word. I'm not a failure and you're not a failure, no matter how much we've messed up. Why? Because God gives us a huge eraser through Jesus Christ and when we make

> GOD GIVES US A HUGE ERASER THROUGH JESUS CHRIST AND WHEN WE MAKE MISTAKES, WE APPLY THE ERASER AND WE CHANGE THE NARRATIVE.

mistakes, we apply the eraser and we change the narrative. We pick ourselves up and we try again!

EVERY FAIL IS ANOTHER OPPORTUNITY

The more we attempt something and fail, the more opportunities we have to succeed. It's easy to assume well-known CEOs, business owners, and innovators always experienced brilliant success. But I learned these people accomplished much more than the average person because they kept going when the average person would've quit.

It's easy to focus on the big result, whether it's a discovery or accomplishment because we usually don't hear about the hundreds of failed attempts beforehand. Failures and setbacks are going to occur as we work towards our goals. Our attitude toward them determines whether we let it stop us or whether we keep going.

PERSEVERANCE

Bill Gates, Albert Einstein, and Walt Disney all had similar approaches to failure. They didn't allow rejection, failure, or obstacles to stop them. Their internal drive and perseverance continually pushed them forward.

Bill Gates' first business was called Traf-O-Data. Believe it or not, he considered it a business failure. But the information he learned from this venture was instrumental in the creation of Microsoft, which eventually turned him into the world's richest man.[1]

Some of Einstein's teachers thought he might be mentally disabled. He was unable to speak fluently until the age of nine. Despite disliking school, he was fascinated with mathematics. Einstein tried to enter the Federal Institute of Technology (FIT) in Zurich, Switzerland, but he failed the entrance examination. Later, he automatically entered into FIT, but he had to take a detour and obtain a diploma from the Cantonal School in Aarau,

Switzerland, first. He later discovered the theory of relativity and is now considered one of the most brilliant minds in history.[2]

Not only did Walt Disney overcome an abusive childhood, but he and his brother's startup cartoon business called Laugh-O-Gram Studios went bankrupt after two years. After this failure, he thought he'd try his hand at acting in Los Angeles but wasn't successful there either. However, while in LA, he noticed there were no cartoon studios out West, so he and his brother started one. He lost legal rights to his first character creation, Oswald the Lucky Rabbit. But instead of fighting back with attorneys, he decided to regroup and start over. What followed was the birth of Mickey Mouse.[3]

In all three examples, they could have gone back home, hung up their hat, and given up. Instead, they didn't. They kept pushing forward and accomplished more than anyone else in their craft because of their mental strength and determination.

After a failure, we often say, *back to square one*. But this is hardly true. We have a huge advantage when we retry because we already know something that doesn't work. Therefore, we learn to approach from a different angle. We can even say our failures lay the groundwork for our successes.

Thomas Edison invented the lightbulb after many failures. If many of us had a fraction of his determination, we'd also do great things. He went in with an interesting, yet inspiring mindset. In response to a question about his missteps, Edison once said, "I have not failed 10,000 times—I've successfully found 10,000 ways that will not work."[4]

He expected failure. Instead of a roadblock, he viewed it as another slight probability of succeeding. He kept trying again and again until he found success. The light bulb eventually came on, and his invention illuminated the world. Edison shows us failure isn't only for weak or stupid people. Geniuses such as Edison fail like everyone else.

I hope this encourages you that failure isn't a bad thing. What *is* a bad thing is throwing in the towel. When you desire something but do nothing, you'll never know if you would've succeeded and how far you could've gone if you'd tried. Also, it's vital to persevere. Success could be right around the corner! Don't quit!

We need not dwell on yesterday's mistakes, but instead, let's look forward to tomorrow's possibilities.

THE POWER OF CONFIDENCE

At a young age, we're told, "You can do or be anything you set your mind to." We tend to hear the, *you can do anything,* part while glossing over the *set your mind to* part. Think about your biggest goal. Maybe it's to be a doctor or a millionaire by age thirty. Maybe it's to get a college scholarship or to be a missionary in a third world country. No matter what your goal is, you'll have obstacles come in your way. Now is the time to make your mind up that you'll do whatever it takes—practice, study, hard work, commitment.

Confidence is a big deal. It can be the difference between one more attempt or quitting. We must keep our eyes on the goal. One defeat can be degrading to our self-esteem and, subsequently, can take a toll on our confidence. Life, however, is full of opportunities. Failure isn't the end of the world. We'll have many chances of redemption to succeed if we don't give up. The question is, do you really want it? Make up your mind.

I love what my middle school band teacher told us about mistakes. He had no opposition to them under one circumstance. He said, "If you're going to make a mistake, make sure it's confident, with a good sound, or then you would be making two mistakes."

YOU LIVE AND YOU LEARN

I took a four-week drivers education class the summer I turned sixteen. The first week, the class consisted of textbook work four hours per day. We didn't sit in the driver's seat until the second week, and then we only drove in twenty-minute stents under the guidance of our instructor.

In the beginning, I made lots of mistakes, such as driving too fast over railroad tracks and taking turns too sharply. The girls in the back didn't appreciate those turns! But I learned and corrected those mistakes in the following days, and my score kept getting better. The last few days, I earned a perfect score, and riding with me was no longer like a miniature roller-coaster ride.

The point is, I got better and more comfortable by actually getting behind the wheel than learning from a textbook about driving. We need to stop hesitating because of the fear of failure. There comes a point where we must push ourselves out of the nests and learn to fly. Sometimes, we have to say: *You know what, I'm going to start and see where it takes me.*

STAY THE COURSE

I played football for one year in the seventh grade, and we did a drill in practice called the Oklahoma drill. In this drill, the offensive player tried to get past the defender on a narrow, in-bound playing field. You were going to hit your opponent no matter what, which was the whole point.

After completing this drill for several weeks, I noticed I did the drill differently based on who my opponent was. When I was up against someone much bigger than me, I didn't run as fast and I braced for the impact of the hit. I wanted to walk away with the least amount of pain as possible.

When doing this, I never gave myself a chance. In my mind, I was already defeated. Therefore, my actions followed suit and down I went. However, when I went up against someone my size, I practiced proper technique and ran full out because I knew I had a good chance of getting past or tackling my opponent. This example shows how much our confidence or fear impacts the outcome of our situations.

It's easiest to work aggressively and with a spirit of excellence when starting something new. We all know the feeling of adrenaline coursing through our blood when a new adventure is at our footsteps. But then the next day hits, and the next day, and so on.

Adrenaline gradually disappears as dread and doubt emerge. It gets harder and harder to have the same aggressive approach as in the beginning. As time passes, our confidence seems to drop when the reality of the struggle gets real.

Life is hard. We will have good days and bad. But it's important to make an intentional effort to overcome struggles and failures. The question remains: *Are we willing to endure more hardship for a chance at success, or are we going to succumb to the struggle and stay defeated?*

Two moving forces produce a greater impact in a collision than a collision with one stationary force. If you're the stationary force, life will control you and beat you down every single time. However, if you're an unrelenting moving force, you can plow through the struggle with momentum and confidence.

I challenge you—stay the course and hit your obstacles head-on.

Reinforcements:

- Failing at something doesn't make you a failure.

- Successful people keep going when the average person would give up.

- Each new attempt is another probability of success.

- We need not dwell on yesterday's mistakes, but instead, look forward to tomorrow's possibilities.

- Our failures lay the groundwork for our successes.

- Are we willing to endure more hardship for a chance at success, or are we going to succumb to the struggle and remain defeated?

Pause and Ponder:

1. How has this chapter altered your perception of failure?

   _____

   _____

   _____

   _____

2. Thinking of an instance where you threw in the towel after failing, how do you think the outcome would've changed if you hadn't given up?

   _____

   _____

   _____

   _____

3. Are you hesitating to do something because you're afraid you'll fail? What's the worst thing that could happen? What if you succeeded?

   _____

   _____

   _____

   _____

18

ESCAPING THE COMFORT ZONE

Remaining in the comfort zone saves energy, it's predictable, and it's safe.

But what if I told you sometimes, we need to leave this instinctive comfort zone?

Research has proven the comfort zone isn't healthy for us to be in 24/7. We could waste years of our life in an autopilot mode and look back with regret because we fell into the mundane and monotony of life. Not only that, many of us would miss our whole purpose in life by remaining in our comfort zones.

Interestingly, according to psychologists, curiosity is linked to happiness. When we refuse to do anything new, we're killing curiosity, and our lives become boring. We begin lacking positive anxiety, known as eustress, which is the good stress that pumps us up. This type of anxiety brings feelings of positive emotions, happiness, and even life satisfaction.[1]

It's a sense of looking forward to the future knowing there's more territory to be discovered, more people to impact, and more songs to be sung. Adventure enriches our souls. Even when we go back into our comfort zone, it gives us more stories to tell and fond memories that make us smile simply thinking about them.

Don't get me wrong—this book is all about setting healthy routines and habits. But I'd be amiss if I didn't encourage spontaneity and adventure. These things are the spice of life. The key is finding balance. Let's explore this a little deeper.

LEAVING THE SAFETY NET

Have you ever watched professional snowboarders? This is an extreme sport in which competitors constantly push the limits to improve. They must learn to leave the comfort zone and resist gravitating back to the familiar. Before Shaun White mastered his infamous double McTwist 1260, a combination of two front flips with three and a half backside spins, he put in countless hours training with airbags and foam pits to cushion the falls until he felt ready to attempt a landing on snow.

But eventually, the moment of truth came where he had to leave the safety nets and put his skill to the test. He had to battle the mindset of failure, knowing he might take many hard hits, bruises, and perhaps an injury. Two weeks before his trip to the Olympics, he had his worst crash ever, planting his face into the wall during practice at the X Games.

"I've paid my dues for that trick, but it's worth it," White said after his crash. "That trick is just a beast of its own, and on some days, it's just tougher than others." [2]

Can you imagine the fear he must have felt attempting the trick again after that brutal face plant? What if he allowed that fear to rule, and he decided to call it quits? He would've missed out on making history. White won the X Games that year and went on to win in Vancouver, too, taking his second consecutive Olympic gold. And his reign at X Games would net him three more gold medals in the next three years -- bringing his consecutive total to six, setting a Winter X Games record.[2]

Likewise, we have a similar choice. We can embrace defeat or embrace the feat. Whichever we choose sets our course, moving us closer to our goals or further away.

In Dreamworks' *Kung Fu Panda*, Master Oogway, the wise turtle, gives advice to Po saying, "Yesterday is history. Tomorrow's a mystery. Today's a gift, and that's why it's called the present."[3] Having this outlook deters thoughts of what we can't control—the past—and

WE CAN EMBRACE DEFEAT OR EMBRACE THE FEAT.

puts the focus on what we can control, the present. Fear will try to stop us in our tracks. Living in the present helps us to keep moving. It allows us to really see and interact with the world around us. When we treat each day as a gift, we don't merely go through the motions, but we start treasuring the moments and making them all count.

Don't take for granted the day ahead of you. Seize every opportunity. Don't let your comfort zone dictate your decisions, restrict your adventure, and take away your freedoms to cultivate and captivate your gifts. You're capable of much more than you realize.

LESSONS FROM NEW EXPERIENCES

Our comfort zone is an invisible boundary of limitation. If we decide to wait until it feels right, we'll most likely never do it.

Perfect opportunities are scarce. There will always be an excuse, whether it's time, money, circumstances, or people that make it reasonable to justify doing nothing. Times like these, we need to stop analyzing and act. Anybody else an overthinker? Sometimes, we need to get over ourselves.

These are great years for us to practice stepping out of our comfort zone. Obligations like career and family only increase as we get older. Taking risks and trying new things now will help us better understand what we like and where our talents lie.

As mentioned, I played football in seventh grade. It wasn't because I wanted to, but mostly because my friends encouraged me to do it with them. The one time I touched the ball all season,

I fumbled. Although I don't regret trying it out, I learned I don't enjoy playing football, nor do I have the talent for it.

I walked away with experiences I'll never forget, and I'll never watch an NFL game and ponder *Hmmm, I wonder if I'd be good or not.* I definitely know that answer now! I also learned many other things that I wouldn't know otherwise, and more importantly, I came out of the cherished comfort zone with a better understanding of who I am.

My two big takeaways that season were persistence and hard work. The motto we chanted after every game and practice was, "Hard work pays off." We put in the work no matter what we were dealing with outside of practice or how much it hurt to hit one more rep or run through one more play. Our comfort zone was challenged daily, and stretching our self-imposed limits made us better. It built backbone and character.

Also, I learned to get hit hard and get right back up. As Rocky Balboa said in Rocky IV, "It isn't how hard you hit; it's about how hard you can get hit and keep moving forward."[4] Strong people can hit hard. But stronger people can get hit and not quit.

So, yeah. I may not have liked or been good at football, but I did learn some valuable life lessons by stepping out and giving it a shot. Trying and failing is better than not doing anything. At least when we try, we know that we went for it and didn't let the opportunity for success pass us.

GROWTH THROUGH DISCOMFORT

Generally speaking, we all like to know what to expect. We like convenience. We want to play it safe. We don't realize how much we love our comfort until it's taken away. It takes great discipline, focus, and determination to choose to get uncomfortable, but it's vital to grow.

I know a family who's vacationed in the same spot for the past ten years. They stay at the same hotel, eat at the same restaurants, and do the same activities year after year. To me, this is incredibly boring. To them, it's comfortable. It creates low stress, but it also stifles adventure and exploration. It hinders new experiences that help expand our horizons and grow.

Life isn't always going to be predictable. We can't always control the outcome. In one form or another, we all will suffer hardships at some point in our lives. Life isn't easy. However, dealing with discomfort and fighting through the pain makes us stronger.

Similarly, to grow a muscle, one must lift more than what the body is comfortable with. The repetition of the exercise results in micro-tears in your muscle fibers. There may be discomfort in that moment and even soreness the next day, but as these tears repair, the muscle grows bigger and stronger.

Muhammed Ali said, "I don't just count my sit-ups; I only start counting when it starts hurting because they're the only ones that count."[5] Developing any skill requires time, effort, and discomfort before we see improvement. Staying near our current skill level wastes our time and inhibits growth. We must push past the pain to reach our goals.

IMPROVING OUR WEAKNESSES

Sometimes, it isn't only important to know what we're good at, but also what needs improving. I've always been introverted, and I've had trouble socializing with people I don't know. I was satisfied with my comfortable circle of friends, with no intention of risking rejection to acquire more.

I often over-analyze situations, and I envision various scenarios of how a future situation will play-out. After a conversation, I always felt like I communicated awkwardly, so I altogether avoided this feeling by only interacting with people I knew.

Years went by, and I never got any better at social interaction. Yet, communication is one of the most important life skills to learn, and I knew I had to improve.

As a self-conscious individual, my number one fear was being embarrassed. I battled this first by engaging in small talk with strangers. Whether it was the grocery store with my mom or another public place, I figured if I did something embarrassing, I'd never see them again, so who cared. Right now, you're either thinking, *Wow, I can totally relate to this,* or, *This dude is crazy.*

By doing this, I gradually got better and more relaxed talking with others, and I eventually progressed to full-on, ordinary conversations with people I had just met. Trust me, I'm not the most socially fluent person in the slightest, but I've come pretty far. But it did take getting out of that debilitating comfort zone.

In school, it's natural for us to spend more time and effort on the classes we enjoy. Sometimes, we must leave what's easy and do what's necessary to improve our overall GPA. This may mean spending more time studying classes we don't like. Whether you love science and hate history or the other way around, you probably need to spend more time studying the subject you don't like.

You would assume since I'm writing a book that I'm an avid reader. Well, not so much. Audiobooks, however, are a Godsend. While reading a book, my mind will often roam thinking about other things. I see words across the page, but I'm not always connecting their meaning with them.

As a result, my reading ACT score is much lower than the other three sections. Although I dislike the reading section much more than the others, I spend the majority of my time studying for the reading section. It's much easier to grow three points in a section with a lower score than improve three points in a higher-scored section.

What are you avoiding because you're bad at it? As we get older and decide on a career path, we can double-down on our strengths, but until then, improve your weaknesses. In doing so, our overall strength will improve so much more.

Brian Tracy, a motivational speaker and self-development author, explains it well. "Move out of your comfort zone. You can only grow if you are willing to feel awkward and uncomfortable when you try something new."[6]

CHALLENGES

When you hear the word challenge, what comes to mind? A dangerous dare, an intimidating obstacle, or a risky move?

For today, I'm going to discuss some healthy challenges to pull you out of your comfort zone, so you'll learn something and grow. There's no opponent in this challenge, only you versus your mind.

Maybe it's talking to one new person a day. Maybe it's reading the Bible every day for the next thirty days. Maybe it's eating healthy for the next six months.

> WHETHER YOU REALIZE IT OR NOT, YOU'VE THE COURAGE TO CONQUER YOUR CHALLENGES.

These things require discipline. They stretch us and make us uncomfortable. Whether you realize it or not, you've the courage to conquer your challenges. You may need to dig deep. Small but continuous improvements are what's important.

If you get 1% better at something each day for a year, you'll end up almost thirty-eight times better by the year-end.[7] Whether you're trying to improve your physical, emotional, mental, or spiritual health, stick to it, stay consistent, and it will pay off.

Write down your healthy challenge to keep you accountable at working on your weaknesses. Keep a journal of your struggle through the process. I'm sure you'll be amazed at what comes out of it.

One YouTube channel, by Matt D'Avella,[8] focuses on minimalism, productivity, and building better habits. He challenges himself with popularized thirty-day challenges. Some examples include, "I started journaling for thirty days," and "I took a cold shower for thirty days," and "I quit caffeine for thirty days."

These fun challenges make life more interesting by testing us mentally, teaching us about ourselves, and seeing how our body adapts to change.

Simple challenges like these make us more flexible because we have trained ourselves to adapt to change. When a real-life challenge presents itself, we'll be cooler, calmer, and more collected.

Also, it tricks our minds into believing change isn't a bad thing. After getting out of our comfort zone once, it's easier the next time.

Leaving your comfort zone may surprise you. Don't wait for the perfect opportunity. Embrace the challenge, and you'll improve your weaknesses, learn, and achieve expectations you never thought were possible.

Reinforcements:

- We can embrace defeat or embrace the feat.
- Our comfort zone is an invisible boundary of limitation.
- Discomfort is necessary for growth.
- Challenge yourself to get out of your comfort zone and try something new daily.
- The more you step out of the comfort zone, the easier it will be.

Pause and Ponder:

1. Are you the type of person who needs to leave their comfort zone more? If so, what's one challenge you can incorporate this week that will take you out of your comfort zone?

   _____

   _____

   _____

   _____

2. What are you avoiding because you're not good at it?
   How can you tackle it and improve this weakness?

   _____

   _____

   _____

   _____

19

WALKING IT OUT

G rowth requires time. The main reason people give up is they don't see overnight success. Consistency is hard to maintain, testing our patience and discipline.

Many times, we get motivated in the beginning and say *I'm going to do (fill in the blank) for four days a week.* We commit to the first week and maybe the second week, but each week after that, it gets harder and harder. We begin saying, *skipping one day won't matter,* or we start questioning whether the goal is worth the struggle anymore. Then, many of us get discouraged and quit.

We must learn to commit and persist through the tough times. Elon Musk, technology entrepreneur, investor, and engineer said, "Persistence is very important. You shouldn't give up unless you are forced to give up."[1] Musk knows what he's talking about after coming back from multiple failures with many of his ventures, including Tesla and SpaceX. He keeps going despite the setbacks and naysayers, and so should we.

1 Corinthians 15:58 advises us well saying, *"Therefore, my beloved brothers, be steadfast, immovable, always abounding in the work of the Lord, knowing that in the Lord your labor is not in vain."* The seed is there even when we don't see the fruit. Keep watering the plant, and in due season, you'll eventually see results.

TRUSTING THE PROCESS

A result can't come without a process, and a process can't be achieved without specific goals. We need specific goals to guide us every step of the way, like a treasure map leading to buried treasure.

As a quick review, we've learned to outline the steps, put them in order, and establish a realistic timeline you think you can accomplish each step. These are your mini-goals. It makes a big achievement possible and not as overwhelming. Focus on one step at a time. Track your progress and reward yourself when you achieve each goal. Before you know it, you'll be celebrating your success.

I've found this system to be the most effective way of staying consistent. My planner also comes in handy. Granted, you do need a good work ethic. Achieving your goals and fulfilling your dreams doesn't come cheaply. You have to put in the work required to get it done. This is grit. You choose whether you have it or not. You can write your vision in your planner all you want, but if you don't run with it, you'll not see it come to pass.

"Write the vision; make it plain on tablets, so he may run who reads it" (Habakkuk 2:2 ESV).

After completing a task, I cross it off. It's very satisfying to mark these mini accomplishments off my list. At the end of each day, I put a large X through the day. I don't know exactly why, but it makes the planner look simpler to me. Plus, it tells me I conquered the day. The day was my target, and I hit the bullseye.

After each week is over, I tear the page out. This lightens the planner and acts to help me remember to *live in what I can control, and not what has already happened.* Each day is a fresh start. That said, some of you need to tear some pages out of your past. Thank God His mercies are new every morning.

I do something similar to help me maintain my consistency with running. I made a mileage chart I place next to the refrigerator. It takes about two seconds each night to write down my daily mileage and a symbol indicating whether I did strength training that day. It keeps me accountable. In season, I'm able to slowly grow my weekly mileage to avoid injury and peak at the right time.

Maybe you're practicing an instrument, learning a new language, or desiring a cleaner diet. You can start using a calendar to check off each day you perform the desired activity. With discipline, it'll become a productive habit. Remember the 21/90 rule? Stay faithful and patient by trusting in the process, which leads to results.

SET REALISTIC EXPECTATIONS

The most important key takeaway about achieving your goals is to make it an attainable process. You must be honest with yourself in developing practical goals and practical ways to accomplish these goals.

I always make sure my goals are hard but realistic. A far-fetched goal will leave you discouraged and cause you to quit. But a goal not challenging enough can also cause you to lose interest and walk away.

The reason many aren't consistent is we develop an unreasonable expectation of what we think we need to do to get to a certain level. Start small and gradually build up until it becomes a daily practice.

IT ALL ADDS UP

You've got to start somewhere, and most things start small. The good news is small, but consistent practices add up. Success is a bunch of little goals adding up to one big goal.

Several girls in my school bring in Starbucks coffee every morning to class. Let's say they cave to this indulgence five days a week. The average cup of coffee is the US is $3 cumulating to $15 weekly or $780 per year.[2] That's not pocket change!

Let's say you want to learn to type and improve your speed. Maybe when you started typing, you could type thirty-six words per minute, but after four weeks of practice, you can type thirty-nine words per minute. Even if it seems small, it's progress and will continue until you stop being consistent. Our bodies continually adapt to become better at what we do daily.

When I look at my eleven-year-old brother, I can't see him growing at a given moment. However, once or twice a year, my mom makes him stand by his growth chart as she draws another line marking his height. Over time, it's easy to see his growth by looking at the previous marks. Lately, he's had a growth spurt, and the change is obvious.

The biggest excuse for not sticking to something is, *I'm so busy, I've got no time.* It's a misconception that we need to spend a great amount of time on something to see growth. If all you have is five to ten minutes, use it. Ten minutes is less than one percent of the day. Sure, maybe it won't make a difference for one day, but over a year, it's almost sixty-one hours. It all adds up.

Zechariah 4:10 says, *"Do not despise these small beginnings, for the Lord rejoices to see the work begin."* You don't have to spend a large amount of time each day on something to see growth and experience its benefits. Persistence is key!

Finding Motivation

Feelings impact the decisions we make. Fear holds us back, and discouragement slows us down. Curiosity takes us out of our comfort zones, and devotion moves us forward. But what happens when our feelings are all over the place?

Sure, we could be super motivated to begin a challenging project after watching Creed or another inspiring movie. We'd be ultra-productive the first week. Then, productivity slows, and we become engulfed in feelings of discouragement. Would you call it quits, or would you keep going?

Even if you don't know your clear destination, simply make progress. We don't always have to see the end from the beginning. The closer we get, the more details we'll be able to make out. Turning back can't be an option. We become more motivated when we know the destination is within our grasp.

My mom grew up on a small horse farm, and she loved to take them out on trail rides. The horses walked at a steady pace and obeyed her commands throughout the journey. They enjoyed the smells, looked at the landscape, and let out a neigh now and then. All of the calmness came to an end right when the horses rounded a corner of dense trees, able to see the house and barn from a distance. The horses knew they were on the home stretch, and they would bolt in a full sprint like they were competing in the Kentucky Derby.

This didn't happen only one time with one horse. It happened every single time with all eight horses. They felt no need to conserve energy because the end is in sight. In a short while, they knew they'd be well-fed, groomed, and able to rest when they made it home.

But what if you're not on the homestretch and the end isn't in sight? One of the best ways to stay dedicated and consistent with things is to establish checkpoints along the way. Instead of waiting until the end result to pat yourself on the back, give yourself rewards along the way. Take a quick breather. This is a good time to regroup and remember what set you on the journey in the first place. But don't camp out here. This is to help you return with renewed motivation to get to the next checkpoint.

Think of it like playing a game of Super Mario Bros. Each world is divided into four sublevels. Each sublevel serves as a checkpoint that, when completed, saves your progress, making you another step closer to conquering that world. There's eight worlds total, and it would be near impossible to beat it one setting. Making it past each checkpoint is much easier than having the final Bowser's Castle in your mind the whole game. And when you encounter defeat, you don't have to start all over every time.

> ONE OF THE BEST WAYS TO STAY DEDICATED AND CONSISTENT WITH THINGS IS TO ESTABLISH CHECKPOINTS ALONG THE WAY.

Seeing our progress keeps us motivated, especially when we start something new. However, we improve the most in the beginning, and we find motivation through the progress we see. In turn, this helps us become more consistent by wanting to get even better. Use your improvement week after week as fuel to keep going.

BUILDING MOMENTUM

Some people call it staying on a roll, getting in the zone, or building momentum. Regardless of what you call it, it's a good indicator someone is making progress. So, how do we get in these hyper-productive states?

Consistency builds momentum. It helps you find your rhythm. A bonfire is easy to maintain after it's already lit. All you need to do is add more wood. But what happens when you stop adding the wood? The fire eventually goes out.

Every day we need to throw another piece of wood into the fire. We can't let our passion burn out. We've got to keep that momentum.

The longer a ball rolls down a hill, the more speed it picks up. Even when the ball must go uphill, it still has leftover momentum to carry it partially up the hill without extra force. Consistency can keep you going even when life gets hard, and you have to start climbing the hill.

Did you know a car is most fuel-efficient when it runs at a consistent speed? A car burns more gas in stop-and-go traffic than staying at a constant speed of 60mph on the highway, even though the vehicle is covering significantly less distance in traffic. The repetitive acceleration and deceleration cause a loss of efficiency. After the car stops at a red light, it takes more kinetic energy to go at a green light than to maintain a consistent speed of 60mph.[3]

Similarly, when we discover our sweet spot, we can hit cruise control. The momentum will keep pushing us forward, and we'll cover much more ground than if we played stop and go with our goals. Eliminate the all-or-nothing attitude and embrace the small steps. Like the tortoise and the hare, slow and steady wins the race.

INCONSISTENCY

We delay our progress when we aren't consistent. It's healthy and refreshing to take short breaks. However, when we aren't moving forward, we're usually moving backward.

Since I wore braces a couple of years ago, I'm now supposed to wear my retainer every night. Honestly, I can usually get by wearing my retainer every other night. But on vacation, I was too lazy to search through my suitcase to find my retainer and missed wearing it for four consecutive nights. I normally can put it on with ease, but it hurt to put it on that fifth night. The next morning, I woke up with extremely sore teeth.

In four nights of neglecting to wear my retainer, my teeth adjusted enough to make it uncomfortable. This is a silly example, but you get the point. Don't be too lazy like I was to do the small thing like searching through my suitcase. If I had gone much longer, my retainer might not have fit at all.

If you've learned a skill, I'm sure you know the importance of staying at least somewhat consistent year-round. Our coaches in track and cross country encourage us to keep running between seasons to maintain our progress. I usually take Sunday off, but I never take more than one day off in a row. From experience, it takes me as many days to build back up that I took off. When you're building a skill, you lose some of your progress if you aren't consistent.

PUSHING PAST TIMES OF SLOW GROWTH

My running journey began for fun in the sixth-grade track season when I really didn't know what I was doing. I decided to do distance running because I was not good at sprinting. To start training, I ran with my mom in our subdivision. In the beginning, I couldn't go far at all without getting a side stitch. If I didn't have my mom for accountability, I probably would've quit because I didn't see any progress, and I was frustrated.

But after a few weeks of pushing past this pain, I never ran with my mom again. She couldn't keep up with me! I got much better, which was the encouragement I needed to become focused and passionate about running.

It's cool to look back on the time when I couldn't even run a mile to see the progress a couple of years later when I won in my age group in a half marathon.

When trying something new, I always try to tell myself to trust the process. There will be highs and lows. There will be times when you see a big spike on the growth chart, and there will be times when it's slow going. During the lows and the slows is when we need to dig deep. Perseverance and persistence will make you unstoppable!

I encourage you to eliminate your excuses, find your rhythm, and stay consistent. Soon enough, you'll start seeing big changes.

Reinforcements:

- Don't expect overnight success. Growth takes time.

- Specific goals are necessary to guide us every step of the way like a treasure map leading to buried treasure.

- Establishing checkpoints as a visual to track our progress keeps us motivated.

- Eliminate the all-or-nothing attitude and embrace the small steps.

- Consistency builds momentum and is critical for success.

- We must push pass the times when we're tempted to quit.

Pause and Ponder:

1. Think of a big goal. What's the best way to measure your progress?

   _____

   _____

   _____

   _____

2. What can you do to maintain motivation and momentum when things get tough?

   _____

   _____

   _____

   _____

20

LIVING PRODUCTIVE

Thanks to God's gift of free-will, we can change parts of our lives we aren't proud of. We mess up every day, but the good news is we can always improve. Our aim isn't perfection, but rather to be better today than we were yesterday. We can stretch beyond our self-perceived limitations to grow into the person God created us to be.

Let's face it. It's going to take effort and purposeful practice to avoid slipping back into our old ways. The first couple of steps will be challenging because we've practiced some of our old bad habits for months or even years.

Building a house is a great analogy for the change that's taking place within us. We're all under construction. It takes the biggest machines such as excavators and bulldozers to ready the ground by removing gigantic rocks and leveling the dirt. Once a solid foundation is prepared and poured, framing will begin to outline the house. The home is starting to take shape.

Thereafter, the central focus begins with plumbing installation, electrical wiring, and HVAC. Insulation and drywall follow, and then the brick is laid outside to strengthen the house.

Our renovation is similar. Removing the dirt and leveling the foundation represents wiping out our old way of living. Fresh new dirt represents our fresh new start and new possibilities. Pouring the foundation represents our commitment to the construction process. There's no turning back now. When Jesus is our foundation, we're unshakable. We then frame our lives with our moral compass. We set boundaries because the word of God is our plumb line.

The plumbing brings a constant flow of living water, promoting growth and freshness. Also, we're wired to the Source. He's our energy. Sparks of joy begin springing up within us. Each brick is another goal set. We become stronger and stronger.

A house built in this manner can withstand any natural disaster, whether it's peer pressure, tragedy, disappointments, setbacks, or failures. Not only that, but we then become a haven for others to turn to for refuge in their times of trouble.

It takes time to build your house the right way. Let's not forget the two little pigs who tried to take the easy way out with sticks and straw. When the big bad wolf came, they couldn't withstand his huff-and-puff power.

"Everyone who hears my teaching and applies it to his life can be compared to a wise man who built his house on an unshakable foundation. When the rains fell and the flood came, with fierce winds beating upon his house, it stood firm because of its strong foundation. But everyone who hears my teaching and does not apply it to his life can be compared to a foolish man who built his house on sand. When it rained and rained and the flood came, with wind and waves beating upon his house, it collapsed and was swept away" (Matthew 7:24-27, TPT).

REMEMBER THE R's

If you're committed to this change, here are five general R's to remember to follow:

- *Responsibility* - You must first take full responsibility for you. Don't blame God, your parents, or any other influences. Leave excuses behind. Taking responsibility for your mistakes is the only way you can grow and learn from them. Accepting responsibility for your future is the only way you'll achieve the goals you've set for yourself. The things that happened to you were out of your control. Let it go, and look forward. You can control your response.

- *Rethink* - Re-examine what you believe in and what you stand for. Why do you think as you do? Is it rooted in ideologies or truth? Is it something someone told you once, and it stuck? If you don't begin to rethink some of your beliefs, you could be believing in something false. For people of faith, our beliefs should be confirmed by the word of God.

- *Reject the old way* - After solidifying your beliefs, walk in them. Reject your old way of thinking. Many times, after setting good habits and establishing firm expectations, you'll find yourself slipping back into the old way and the old mindsets. This could be a struggle for a while but stay consistent. You'll overcome it.

- *Renew your mind* - Think excellence. Think honor. Think truth. Don't follow the ways of the world but be continually transformed by meditating on God's word. Get it from your head into your heart. Proverbs 23:7 tells us, *"As a man thinks in his heart, so is he."*

- *Resound* - Speak with your actions, so they resound into your atmosphere. Declare life into the dry and desolate places. Decree that you're a difference-maker. Be the soul on fire that ignites a spark into everyone they meet.

THE FINAL HUDDLE

Wow! What a great journey we've been on! We've covered so much ground from finding our identity and time management to handling addiction and facing failure. I hope you've taken away some golden nuggets to enrich your soul but also to enrich your entire life and those around you.

We may be parting ways for a season, but your journey doesn't end here. From this point, all it takes is practice, consistency, and trusting God to transform you into the person He created you to be. And you were created for greatness!

> YOU HAVE BIG POTENTIAL, AND GOD HAS AMAZING PLANS FOR YOU.

Take a minute and think about your biggest takeaways. Ask God how to implement them into your life best. You have big potential, and God has amazing plans for you. I have faith you'll stay the course and fulfill all His promises He's spoken over you.

I don't expect you to remember every detail or statistic in this book. However, I do hope you'll remember how this book made you feel. I hope you feel *valuable* because you're chosen by God to accomplish awesome things. I hope you feel *mighty* because through Christ Jesus, you're more than a conqueror. I hope you feel *empowered* because you've been given powerful tools to succeed in life.

Sadly, I also know these feelings may fade. The good news is the discipline you're establishing will enable you to continue doing what you know is right even when you don't feel like it. It sets your face like flint. You won't be ruled by emotions but by a greater power that's within you. Don't waver because if God is for you who can be against you?

If it makes you feel better, I've learned almost every concept written in this book through failure. I'm not perfect. I haven't nailed every aspect of growing up as a teen, but I do know I'm heading in the right direction. I hope I can save you from making some of the same mistakes I made.

Also, I realize some of these topics may have made you uncomfortable, and that's completely okay. The uncomfortable feeling is the right sign toward your first step to change. Setting good habits won't only better yourself but will also better the lives around you.

Making progress isn't easy. Expect setbacks. Expect rejection. But never expect to give up. No matter what, never back down. Keep your eyes on the goal and push yourself closer each day.

Setting good habits produces perseverance, even in hard times. Perseverance refines our character. And a proven character always leads us back to hope, which never disappoints. Don't get distracted and drift out of your lane. Stay the course, friend, and always keep moving.

I hope to have somehow ignited a spark or fanned the flame within you. If I've motivated you at all, I encourage you to keep the fire burning. It's easy for us to get pumped up for a few weeks, and when life gets in the way, we deflate.

Many people start, but few people finish. If it were easy everyone would do it. This is where the rubber meets the road. This is where we push through until we breakthrough. I urge you, don't give up!

Remember, the first step is all it takes. Live for God and do what you're passionate about, and everything else will fall into place. You're special, and God made you for a reason. Use your gifts to further His kingdom and be bold despite other opinions. You aren't alone in your struggles or your victories.

So, if you've learned anything, know you're loved, God has big plans for you, and through Him you can have an abundant life.

It's time to be resolute, strong, and extremely courageous! No longer will we be compromised by the culture around us.

We will be torchbearers!
We will be trendsetters!
We will be trailblazers!

Our destinies are worth fighting for. We won't settle for good enough. We won't take better. We'll fight for what's best! Let's arise as a bold new army of Christ-followers that won't only take the city but take the land as well! Are you with me?

BONUS
TIPS FOR SCHOOL

[Disclaimer: Since this book is all about self-development, it's important for me to reveal some of the strategies I've learned. So, for your reference, I've added an exclusive bonus chapter, *Tips for School*. I hope you find it helpful!]

* * *

School is tough. However, it's easier and much more enjoyable when you develop the right study methods that work for you. These tips center around study habits, organization skills, and test-taking pointers. Discovering the right tricks can drastically improve your educational experience and set you up for success for years to come. In no particular order, here are a few of my secrets.

1. GET TO KNOW YOUR TEACHERS.

Every teacher has a different teaching style and classroom policy. Some teachers are strict, while others are more laid-back. Know what you can and can't do in each class to avoid getting in trouble. You definitely don't want to be on the teacher's bad side.

You don't have to be the teacher's pet, but you genuinely do want to be liked by your teachers, especially in highly subjective classes. He/she will likely be more lenient to a student who they know studies hard and cares about their grade.

So, how do I get favor from my teachers? Great question. The best way is to show you care about the class and its content. Always be respectful and obey the rules of the classroom. Occasionally, sincerely ask how the teacher's day is going and participate in class. Show the teacher you're there to work hard and learn, not to talk and waste time.

Also, be honest with your teacher if you don't understand something. Ask questions, even if it may seem like a dumb question. Any good teacher wants you to understand the topic and will be willing to stay a few minutes after class to help you.

I used to avoid asking questions because I was afraid the students would think I'm a stupid or a nerd. There's nothing wrong with admitting that you don't understand something. It reveals courage and teachers love to help those students who're also willing to help themselves.

2. Prioritize Your Classes.

Sadly, the class you most enjoy probably isn't necessarily the class you should spend the most time on. If you're concerned about your grades, you probably need to spend more time on the classes you're not doing as well in.

Therefore, it's important to prioritize.

You might have a 99% in math, 89% in history, and have a project due the next day in both classes. You may love math and hate history, but it would be wiser to spend more time to meet the rubric of the history project and make sure it's excellent before you begin on the math project.

Also, you're freshest and most alert when you first sit down to study. If you have homework from multiple classes to tackle, I recommend starting with your hardest class. Save the easier classes that you can perform on autopilot with less brainpower last.

3. RESIST PROCRASTINATION.

We naturally feel like we have more time than we actually do. When you start on a project early and do a little, bit-by-bit, the quality of the work will improve, and you'll be much less stressed.

Say you have to memorize seventy-five Spanish words by Friday. It's much more manageable to learn twenty-five new words Monday, Tuesday, and Wednesday night. Spend Thursday night reviewing all the words and focus on the ones you're struggling with. Trying to learn seventy-five words on Thursday night would be much more stressful, and I guarantee you wouldn't do as well on the test.

Trust me, studying in small segments is much better than cramming last minute. Your health and your grade will thank you!

Successful people always ponder what they can do today to make tomorrow slightly better and less stressful.

4. SHOW UP READY TO GO.

Attendance is crucial. Never underestimate the significance of simply being present. It's incredibly difficult to catch up when you miss class, and you'll never know what you missed. You may receive the handout, but you missed the valuable instruction that went with it.

The stress of catching up isn't worth it. I advise you only to miss school if you absolutely must.

Also, when you show up, come prepared physically and mentally. Have your books, pencils, and other necessary materials. Be ready to learn, engage, and work hard.

5. TAKE GOOD NOTES.

This can apply to every class, but I feel this skill has helped me the most in history and science (mostly fact-based classes, although it's useful in conceptual and application classes too).

When taking notes of a presentation, I never write it word for word like I used to. Notes should be bulleted. Also, only write what you don't know or what's important. This saves time and makes it easier to study.

As long as they're legible, don't worry about your notes being messy. This allows you to write faster. But also listen and think about what you're writing.

Use shorthand or abbreviations whenever possible to also save time when taking notes. Learn shorthand if you can. Otherwise, if your abbreviation makes sense to you, go with it. Keep in mind your notes are for *your* benefit.

Even if the teacher doesn't tell you to take notes, you may want to anyway. The simple act of writing something down improves your chances of remembering it. Some people may benefit from re-writing their notes as an added study tool.

6. STAY ORGANIZED.

It would be best if you were organized both mentally and physically for school. Knowing where everything is located is a huge time saver.

Your mind is kind of like an office. You may have only a couple of papers out on your desk at a time, but the rest is filed orderly in cabinets or drawers. However, if every paper was lying haphazardly on your desk, there's no way you could work effectively and find the one paper you need. If you're unorganized, you might spend more time searching for the paper than working on it.

I highly recommend a good planner. This helps me remember my passwords for accounts and assists with my mental organization.

I have a good memory, but I always write down what I need to remember, and I prioritize it. This is my way of organizing my thoughts into filing cabinets in alphabetical order. At a glance, I see what needs to be done and focus on the next task on my list.

When it comes to physical organization, less is better. There's no right way to organize. If you can remember where you put things, then you should consistently put it there each time. It's easier to carry a fewer number of folders or papers.

For example, my teachers last year in Biology, Chemistry, History, and Latin didn't give an absurd amount of papers. Because of this, I combined the papers in Biology and Chemistry into one binder and I put History and Latin in another folder. In the binder, I used the first two tabs for Biology and the next two for chemistry. In the folder, I used the right side for History and the left side for Latin. To declutter, after each semester, I put all the papers I didn't need for the next semester in a drawer in case I needed to refer back to them.

7. LEARN FROM YOUR MISTAKES.

There will be times in school when you aren't proud of your performance. I know I've had my fair share of bombed tests and assessments.

If we have poor grades or test scores, we need to uncover the reason we did poorly instead of beating ourselves up over it. Ask yourself three questions. *How did I prepare for this? How hard have I been working in this class? What will I do differently in the future?* Then, implement this change next time.

Reflection is always beneficial, whether you performed good or bad.

You could pose these same three questions even if you did great on the test. Then all you need to do is repeat the same process. As the saying goes, "Don't try fixing something that ain't broken."

8. FIND STUDY METHODS THAT WORK FOR YOU.

Several study strategies have worked for me, including looking over my notes, reading them out loud, making notecards so I can quiz myself, using study apps or quiz apps, watching YouTube instructional videos, and taking practice tests. It usually depends on the class and the topic as to which strategy I use.

For example, when studying a new language, I primarily use notecards to memorize new words and recite them out loud. For English, practice tests work the best for me. For math, it's all about practice and memorizing formulas using flashcards. However, I often refer to YouTube videos if I'm having trouble figuring out a math problem in calculus. For history, I do a combination of these things, but I found videos help a lot.

Don't limit yourself to only one learning method. The more you can use, the better.

When given a new music piece in band, it was crucial to use many methods to become familiar with the piece and learn the rhythms, tempo, and how to play it. Most of the time, we first listened to a recording by professionals on how the piece should sound. Then, we listened to a metronome to gauge the rhythm, first starting slower, then worked up to the actual speed. We worked on the rhythm through silent-playing certain sections by blowing air through the instrument or clapped certain difficult rhythms. We worked on the piece individually, as a section, and with the whole band. We played the piece through, then focused on specific lines or parts that were more difficult. We tuned our instrument to make sure our sound was right and synced with the band.

We had one of the best middle school bands in the state, and we used over ten methods to learn difficult music and perform it exceptionally. Depending on your upcoming test or whatever you want to learn, sometimes one study method will be enough. In some cases, three, five, seven, or even ten study methods might work for you.

9. Minimize Distractions.

Find a quiet area to study. When I study or do homework, I only have that class's homework on my desk. This makes it less overwhelming than if all my homework is lined up in front of me.

Also, try to avoid having your cell phone in the room with you unless necessary to do your work. If TV and music are distracting, turn it off as well.

10. TAKE PRACTICE TESTS.

Sometimes, I struggle with test anxiety, and being super-nervous before tests isn't helpful. It becomes an even bigger problem when our nervous level is in direct proportion to the importance of the exam.

I find taking practice tests is the best way for me to not be as nervous for exams—especially on standardized tests. It gives me an idea of what the content will be like on the real test, it helps my pacing, and practice tests give me a good idea of what score I'll receive on the actual test.

I have an idea of how much I should study and also what sections or problems I should spend more time looking over. If you can focus on the questions you missed and understand why you missed them, then you'll improve significantly.

By taking practice tests, I'm more confident and less nervous in the actual test. I know I'm prepared, and I know I've practiced enough to perform well.

Practice tests can often be found online.

11. GO IN WITH A NEW PERSPECTIVE.

If all you can think about is how much you hate school, then you'll hate it even more. I know it's hard to do, but try to enjoy it and see what happens. Approach school from a new perspective.

What has worked for me is viewing my grades as a challenge, not something to stress out over. As a competitive person, I love challenges, and I hate to lose. I applied this competitive trait to school, and it has helped me tremendously.

After each test, try to compete with yourself for the next one. When we see ourselves growing, we'll be motivated to improve even more. I've learned that competing with yourself is better than competing with others. Competition with others in this manner never brings out the best in me. I'll either settle at the top and not push myself further or quit at the bottom, thinking there's no way I'll ever reach the top or even average. However, when I compete with myself, I know I can always improve, and I find it rewarding to measure my growth from the previous assessment.

Don't stress about school and take it too seriously. Find a balance between when to be serious and when to talk and have fun. Sure, school matters, but don't beat yourself up over one letter grade. In the larger scheme of things, you'll look back and probably wish you enjoyed school more. I'm halfway done with high school, and I've seen too many of my peers stressed, letting school affect their emotional health.

Grades don't define you. Doing your best is the best you can do. Remember, we're all gifted with different traits and abilities.

12. WORK HARD.

There's no way to overlook this one. If you want to succeed, you must work for it. Some people are naturally more driven than others. However, developing a good work ethic is important for everyone. I've worked hard in my education, and I've performed better than others who are naturally more gifted than me.

I guarantee my natural IQ intelligence is no higher than many of my peers, but I push myself to get better. There's nothing wrong with being a *try-hard*. I'd rather be known as a *try-hard* than lazy. Those people who label you as such are probably jealous that you push yourself to get better and leave them behind. Many want what you've got, but they don't want to put in the work you did.

A good work ethic is an admirable trait to acquire. When you work hard and aspire to do great, you'll do well in school, and you can apply it to everything else outside school.

Proverbs 12:11 says, *"Those who work their land will have abundant food, but those who chase fantasies have no sense."* Hard work pays off.

13. USE PLAY-ON-WORDS TO REMEMBER THINGS.

This is something that helps me classify information to remember for an assessment.

For example, we had to know about a famous geologist named James Hutton and his theory of uniformitarianism. He believed the earth was ancient, and changes on the earth occurred slowly and gradually.

To link the name with his belief, our teacher helped us with a saying. "James Hutton believed the earth was puttin' along." It may be corny, but what matters is that it gets the job done. Maybe a little too well, ... I took that class two years ago!

14. VERBALLY COMMUNICATE CONTENT WITH SOMEONE ELSE.

You can reaffirm you know the content when you can explain and teach it to someone else. This not only helps the other person understand it, but it also reveals to you what you know or don't know.

It's also good practice for free-response questions on exams because you'll have to explain the answer on paper. Another similar way my teacher, Mrs. Lovely, taught me is to ask a question, get the answer, and follow back with, "So, [repeat the answer]."

I admit, sometimes, I'd nod my head to the teacher after getting an answer because I was too embarrassed to ask a second time if I didn't get it. This process allows the teacher to confirm your knowledge that you understand what you asked and will enable you to remember it without having to ask an awkward second question. If you can't explain the content back to the teacher or someone else, you don't know it and need to go over it again.

15. CRAM THE SMART WAY.

Most tests we take in school have some aspect of memorization and recall. What I've learned to do is cram about three of the hardest pieces of information into your head right before the test or quiz begins. Keep on saying them in your head until you get the test, then quickly write them down in the corner of your test paper. Then, you can go back to reference those for the questions. It's a pretty simple method, but it works. It's like getting two or three free answers from the start.

Currently, I use this strategy for difficult formulas in calculus and difficult pieces of information in US history.

This is the only form of cramming that I advocate.

16. FIND A GO-TO GROUP PROJECT PARTNER.

I recommend picking someone who you work well with and who'll help you get a good grade, even if you don't know them well. I've learned it's easy to get sidetracked when working with friends.

It's never fun when you get stuck with someone and have to do 90% of the project alone to get a decent grade. If you've a friend you know you can work well with, that's great. However, if not, get out of your comfort zone and make new friends. It's an added bonus if they're smart.

17. DON'T BE AFRAID TO ASK QUESTIONS.

If you're working on homework and you run into something you don't understand, call up a classmate and ask for help. Often, they'll be honored you came to them with your question, and they'll be eager to offer you help.

This takes swallowing some pride, but it's saved me a few times. I'm sure you'll have an opportunity to return the favor.

18. If You're Offered to Take Advanced Classes, Take Them.

This is especially important if you plan on going to college. My experience might be different than yours, but in my eighth-grade year, I was invited into the Cohort (Advanced Scholars) program. I questioned my abilities and if it might be too rigorous but decided to go for it.

Schools aren't going to invite people to fail the program. If they invite you, I'm sure you can do it. We often don't give ourselves enough credit.

Honestly, it hasn't been as hard as I thought it would be. I like it because I'm in classes with other like-minded students, 90% of them are hardworking, friendly, and good influences.

The great thing about the program is I can get college credit for my classes by passing an end-of-the-year AP exam. This saves time and my parent's wallet. I finished sophomore year, and I've accumulated three college credits already.

19. Focus on Learning, Not the Grade.

Sure, grades are important, and we should care about them. But sometimes, we forget about the process leading to good grades.

If all you're focusing on is the grade, you may get it, but more than likely you won't remember the content for long. When I fall into this trap, I find myself doing a brain dump right after the exam, forgetting everything I studied. This doesn't benefit me long-term.

However, when you have a passion for learning, your grades will, by default, improve.

If we focus on learning the material and improving our skills, we will inevitably receive better grades.

20. PRAY AND TRUST GOD.

"Do not yield to fear, for I am always near. Never turn your gaze from me, for I am your faithful God. I will infuse you with my strength and help you in every situation. I will hold you firmly with my victorious right hand" (Isaiah 41:10 TPT).

APPENDIX A:
HELP HOTLINES FOR TEENS

ADDICTION, DRUGS AND ALCOHOL
SAMHSA (Substance Abuse and Mental Health Services Administration), 1-800-662-4357
Drug Abuse National Helpline, 1-800-662-4357

BULLYING AND CYBERBULLYING
CyberTipline, 24/7, US, 1-800-843-5678
National Bullying Prevention, www.Pacer.org
StopBullying.gov

CRISIS HELP
Biblical help for youth in crisis, 1-800-HIT-HOME
Youth Crisis Hotline, 1-800-448-4663
Teen Hope Line, 1-800-394-HOPE
Prayer and General Counseling www.prayerandhope.org, 1-866-599-2264

EATING DISORDERS
Eating Disorders Awareness and Prevention, 1-800-931-2237
Eating Disorders Center, 1-888-236-1188
National Association of Anorexia Nervosa and Associated Disorders, 1-847-831-3438

MENTAL HEALTH
National Alliance on Mental Illness, 1-800-950-NAMI (6264)

New Hope Telephone Counseling Center, 1-714-NEW-HOPE (639-4673)
SAMHSA (Substance Abuse and Mental Health Services Administration), 1-800-662-4357

PORN ADDICTION
Fireproof Ministries, www.fireproofministries.com/pornaddiction
Covenant Eyes, www.covenanteyes.com and their supporting links
Be Free in Christ, www.befreeinchrist.com

SALVATION
Grace Help Line 24 Hour Christian Service, 1-800-982-8032
Want to know Jesus? 1-888-NEED-HIM

SUICIDE
Emergency, dial 911
National Suicide Prevention Lifeline, 1-800-273-TALK (8255)
National Hopeline Network, 1-800-784-2433 (1-800-SUICIDE), www.hopeline.com

APPENDIX B: SALVATION

1. **Salvation is a Gift.**

Ephesians 2:8-9. *"For by grace you have been saved through faith; and that not of yourselves, it is the gift of God; not as a result of works, that no one should boast."*

2. **Sin Separates.**

Romans 3:23. *"For all have sinned and fall short of the glory of God."*

Acts 3:19. *"Repent therefore and return, that your sins may be wiped away, in order that times of refreshing may come from the presence of the Lord."*

3. **The One True God.**

Acts 4:12. *"And there is salvation in no one else; for there is no other name under heaven that has been given among men by which we must be saved."*

John 14:6. *"Jesus said to him, 'I am the way, and the truth, and the life; no one comes to the Father but through Me.'"*

4. **Confess and Believe.**

Romans 10:9-10. *"That if you confess with your mouth Jesus as Lord, and believe in your heart that God raised Him from the dead, you shall be saved; for with the heart a person believes, resulting in righteousness, and with the mouth he confesses, resulting in salvation."*

John 3:16. *"For God so loved the world, that He gave His only begotten Son, that whoever believes in Him should not perish, but have eternal life."*

5. **New Life.**

2 Corinthians 5:17. *"Therefore if anyone is in Christ, he is a new creature; the old things passed away; behold, new things have come."*

SALVATION PRAYER

Have you ever made Jesus the Lord and Savior of your life?

If not, I encourage you to pray this prayer and start a new life in Christ.

Dear God,

I come to You in the Name of Jesus. I admit that I am not right with You, and I want to be right with You. I ask You to forgive me of all my sins. The Bible says if I confess with my mouth that "Jesus is Lord," and believe in my heart that God raised Him from the dead, I will be saved. (Romans 10:9) I believe with my heart, and I confess with my mouth that Jesus is the Lord and Savior of my life. Thank You for saving me! I dedicate my life to You.

In Jesus' Name I pray. Amen.

If you prayed this prayer for the first time, I'd like to know. Please send me an email at noahhalloran1@gmail.com.

APPENDIX C: NOTES

PART 1: LAUNCH

Chapter 1: Forming Habits

1. Satterfield, Jamie. "Attorney: Teens' Charges in Fatal Gatlinburg Fire Dropped." Knoxville News Sentinel. Knoxville, July 5, 2017. https://www.knoxnews.com/story/news/local/tennessee/gatlinburg/2017/06/30/att orney-arson-charges-against-teens-fatal-gatlinburg-wildfire-dropped/442706001/. Accessed 6/23/19.

Chapter 2: Defining Success

1. Baer, Drake. "How 9 Incredibly Successful People Define Success." Business Insider. Business Insider, June 2, 2014. https://www.businessinsider.com/how-9-incredibly-successful-people-define-success-2014-5#popular-author-stephen-covey-said-that-the-definition-of-success-is-deeply-individual-9.

2. Vaughn, Kassandra. "You Will Spend 90,000 Hours of Your Lifetime at Work. Are You Happy?" Medium. Medium, May 5, 2018. https://medium.com/@KassandraVaughn/you-will-spend-90-000-hours-of-your-lifetime-at-work-are-you-happy-5a2b5b0120ff.

3. Richard II: Entire Play. Accessed December 30, 2019. http://shakespeare.mit.edu/richardii/full.html.

4. Lparmerter. "It's Surprising How Often Americans Change Jobs!" WZOZ 103.1, October 3, 2018. https://wzozfm.com/its-surprising-how-often-americans-change-jobs/.

5. "Harold S. Kushner Quotes (Author of When Bad Things Happen to Good People)." Goodreads. Goodreads. Accessed December 10, 2019. https://www.goodreads.com/author/quotes/26180.Harold_S_Kushner.

Chapter 3: Training to Be Disciplined

1. Smith-Strickland, Kiona. "How Ships Survive a Hurricane at Sea." Popular Mechanics. June 5, 2004. Accessed 9/9/19.

2. "Eddie Lacy Is More than a Meme." ESPN. ESPN Internet Ventures. Accessed December 31, 2019. http://www.espn.com/espn/feature/story/_/id/20756278/seattle-seahawks-eddie-lacy-opens-public-struggle-weight.

3. Taylor, James. "How Britain Hoped to Avoid War with Germany In The 1930s." Imperial War Museums. Accessed December 31, 2019. https://www.iwm.org.uk/history/how-britain-hoped-to-avoid-war-with-germany-in-the-1930s.

4. Beck, Julie. "The Running Conversation in Your Head." The Atlantic. Atlantic Media Company, November 23, 2016. https://www.theatlantic.com/science/archive/2016/11/figuring-out-how-and-why-we-talk-to-ourselves/508487/.

5. Gil, Rodrigo. "'If You Don't Rule Your Mind, It Will Rule You.'" Medium. Medium, December 3, 2017. https://medium.com/@rodrigogil_88321/if-you-dont-rule-your-mind-it-will-rule-you-b8b315ba6e73.

6. "Excuses Quotes (369 Quotes)." Goodreads. Goodreads. Accessed December 31, 2019. https://www.goodreads.com/quotes/tag/excuses.

7. Covey, Stephen R. 7 Habits of Highly Effective People: Powerful Lessons in Personal Change. S.1: Simon & Schuster, 2020.

Chapter 4: Discovering Your Identity

1. Conger, Cristen. "How Accurate Is Our Mental Image of Ourselves?" HowStuffWorks Science. HowStuffWorks, March 8, 2018. https://science.howstuffworks.com/life/inside-the-mind/human-brain/mental-image.htm.

2. YouTube. YouTube. Accessed January 1, 2020. https://www.youtube.com/channel/UCR0VLWitB2xM4q7tjkoJUPw.

3. YouTube. YouTube, December 29, 2017. https://www.youtube.com/watch?v=KjJXB2Zkxgo.

4. "Impact of Fire on Soil Life and Nutrients: NSW Department of Primary Industries." Industry and Investment NSW. Accessed September 13, 2019. https://www.dpi.nsw.gov.au/content/archive/agriculture-today-stories/ag-today-archives/agriculture_today_february_2006/2006-002/columns/impact_of_fire_on_soil_life_and_nutrients.

Chapter 5: Winning the Mind Game

1. "A Quote by Henry Ford." Goodreads. Goodreads. Accessed June 24, 2019. https://www.goodreads.com/quotes/978-whether-you-think-you-can-or-you-think-you-can-t--you-re.

2. "Can We Ever Stop Thinking?" LiveScience. Purch. Accessed November 21, 2019. https://www.livescience.com/can-you-ever-stop-thinking.html.

3. Englishbookgeorgia.com. Accessed August 7, 2019. https://englishbookgeorgia.com/blogebg/thomas-edison-mothers-letter-changed-the-world/.

4. "The Story of a Mom That Raised the Inventor of The Light Bulb..." The Story of Thomas Edison And How His Mother Was the Making of Him. Accessed August 16, 2019. https://www.childrenlearningreading.org/blog/thomas-edison-story.html.

5. "A Quote from Winnie the Pooh Library." Goodreads. Goodreads. Accessed August 16, 2019. https://www.goodreads.com/quotes/6659295-you-are-braver-than-you-believe-stronger-than-you-seem.

6. Smith, Stew. "The Mind and Body Connection." Military.com. Accessed November 21, 2019. https://www.military.com/military-fitness/health/the-mind-and-body-connection.

7. Reber, Paul. "What Is the Memory Capacity of the Human Brain?" Scientific American, May 1, 2010. Accessed November 21, 2019. https://www.scientificamerican.com/article/what-is-the-memory-capacity/.

8. "Tips for Athletes Looking to 'Get in the Zone.'" The Sports Doc Chalk Talk with Dr. Chris Stankovich. Accessed November 21, 2019. https://drstankovich.com/tips-for-athletes-looking-to-get-in-the-zone/.

9. Catalyst. "Believe and Achieve: Confidence Linked to Academic Success." CATALYST. CATALYST, February 15, 2016. Accessed November 22, 2019. http://utcatalyst.org/blog/2016/02/15/believe-and-achieve-confidence-linked-to-academic-success.

10. "Decades of Scientific Research That Started a Growth Mindset Revolution." The Growth Mindset - What is Growth Mindset - Mindset Works. Accessed November 22, 2019. https://www.mindsetworks.com/science/.

11. Quoteresearch, Author. "Everybody Is a Genius. But If You Judge a Fish by Its Ability to Climb a Tree, It Will Live Its Whole Life Believing That It Is Stupid." Quote

Investigator, July 31, 2019. https://quoteinvestigator.com/2013/04/06/fish-climb/.

Chapter 6: Taking a Leap of Faith

1. "Hebrew Roots/The Original Foundation/Faith." Hebrew Roots/The original foundation/Faith - Wikibooks, open books for an open world. Accessed July 13, 2019. https://en.wikibooks.org/wiki/Hebrew_Roots/The_original_foundation/Faith.

2. *Horton Hears a Who!* New York: Random House, 1992.

3. Heimbuch, Jaymi. "13 Facts to Change the Way You See Elephants." MNN. Mother Nature Network, August 9, 2019. https://www.mnn.com/earth-matters/animals/photos/12-facts-change-way-see-elephants/elephants-can-hear-through-their-feet.

4. The Hunger Games (Film)." Wikipedia. Wikimedia Foundation, November 29, 2019. https://en.wikipedia.org/wiki/The_Hunger_Games_(film).

5. "The Hunger Games." IMDb. IMDb.com. Accessed December 6, 2019. https://www.imdb.com/title/tt1392170/characters/nm0000661.

6. "Rick Warren: Why God Encourages Christians to 'Fear Not' 365 Times in the Bible." The Christian Post. The Christian Post. Accessed December 7, 2019. https://www.christianpost.com/news/rick-warren-why-god-encourages-christians-to-fear-not-365-times-in-the-bible.html.

PART 2: LEAD

1. YouTube. YouTube. Accessed January 5, 2020. https://www.youtube.com/watch?v=gMFc7agO09w.

Chapter 7: Setting Priorities

1. Saff, Science X. "Texting Increases Crash Risk 23 Times: Study." Phys.org. Phys.org, July 28, 2009. https://phys.org/news/2009-07-texting.html.

2. Larkin, Bob, and Bob Larkin. "20 Facts That Will Make You So Happy You're Not a Teen Right Now." Best Life, November 5, 2019. https://bestlifeonline.com/teen-facts/.

3. "A Quote by Roy E. Disney." Goodreads. Goodreads. Accessed January 5, 2020. https://www.goodreads.com/quotes/661305-it-s-not-hard-to-make-decisions-once-you-know-what.

Chapter 8: Managing Time

1. YouTube. YouTube. Accessed November 27, 2019. https://www.youtube.com/watch?v=LrRfjmv-5cQ.

2. "A Quote by Muhammad Ali." Goodreads. Goodreads. Accessed November 27, 2019. https://www.goodreads.com/quotes/200873-don-t-count-the-days-make-the-days-count.

3. Prossack, Ashira. "This Year, Don't Set New Year's Resolutions." Forbes. Forbes Magazine, January 1, 2019. https://www.forbes.com/sites/ashiraprossack1/2018/12/31/goals-not-resolutions/#4d4e8f273879.

4. "The Most Popular 2019 New Year's Resolutions." Vitagene, December 19, 2018. https://vitagene.com/blog/most-popular-2019-new-years-resolution/.

Chapter 9: Minimizing Stress

1. "Charles R. Swindoll Quotes (Author of The Grace Awakening)." Goodreads. Goodreads. Accessed December 21, 2019. https://www.goodreads.com/author/quotes/5139.Charles_R_Swindoll.

2. "Exercise and Stress: Get Moving to Manage Stress." Mayo Clinic. Mayo Foundation for Medical Education and Research, March 8, 2018. https://www.mayoclinic. org/healthy-lifestyle/stress-management/in-depth/ exercise-and-stress/art-20044469.

Chapter 10: Resting Properly

1. YouTube. YouTube. Accessed December 21, 2019. https:// www.youtube.com/watch?v=GLcJHC9J7l4.

2. "Sleep for Teenagers." National Sleep Foundation. Accessed December 21, 2019. https://www.sleepfoundation.org/ articles/teens-and-sleep.

3. "How and Why Using Electronic Devices at Night Can Interfere With Sleep." National Sleep Foundation. Accessed January 5, 2020. https://www.sleepfoundation.org/articles/ why-electronics-may-stimulate-you-bed.

4. "Showing All Quotes That Contain 'Demetri Martin'." Goodreads. Goodreads. Accessed December 21, 2019. https://www.goodreads.com/quotes/ search?page=3&q=demetri+martin.

5. HiKabir. "Stanford Professor: Working This Many Hours a Week Is Basically Pointless. Here's How to Get More Done-by Doing Less." CNBC. CNBC, March 21, 2019. https://www.cnbc.com/2019/03/20/stanford-study-longer- hours-doesnt-make-you-more-productive-heres-how- to-get-more-done-by-doing-less.html.

6. Popely, Rick. "If Premium Gas Is Recommended for My Car, Will Using Regular Void the Warranty, Ruin the Engine?: News from Cars.com." Cars.com, January 31, 2018. https://www.cars.com/articles/if-premium-gas-is- recommended-for-my-car-will-using-regular-void- the-warranty-ruin-the-engine-1420684149253/.

7. "A Quote by Denzel Washington." Goodreads. Goodreads. Accessed December 21, 2019. https://www.goodreads.com/quotes/9450482-just-because-you-are-doing-a-lot-more-doesn-t-mean.

8. Rinkesh. "Advantages and Disadvantages of Crop Rotation." Conserve Energy Future, June 1, 2018. https://www.conserve-energy-future.com/advantages-disadvantages-crop-rotation.php.

9. "World Population History." World Population. Accessed December 21, 2019. https://worldpopulationhistory.org/map/2012/mercator/1/0/25/.

Chapter 11: Handling Addiction

1. "Addiction." Merriam-Webster. Merriam-Webster. Accessed December 21, 2019. https://www.merriam-webster.com/dictionary/addiction.

2. "Top 12 Teen Addictions: Addiction Expert Scott Gallagher." Teen Drug Rehabs, August 6, 2013. Accessed November 12, 2019. https://www.teendrugrehabs.com/blog/top-12-teen-addictions-according-to-teen-addicts-themselves/.

3. "Teen Behavioral Addictions Treatment." Paradigm Malibu, October 19, 2018. Accessed November 13, 2019. https://paradigmmalibu.com/teen-behavioral-addictions-treatment/.

4. Hurley, Katie. "Teenage Cell Phone Addiction: Are You Worried About Your Child?" Psycom.net - Mental Health Treatment Resource Since 1986. Accessed November 13, 2019. https://www.psycom.net/cell-phone-internet-addiction.

5. Swns. "Americans Check Their Phones 80 Times a Day: Study." New York Post. New York Post,

November 8, 2017. https://nypost.com/2017/11/08/
americans-check-their-phones-80-times-a-day-study/.

6. McSpadden, Kevin. "Science: You Now Have a Shorter
   Attention Span Than a Goldfish." Time. Time, May 14,
   2015. https://time.com/3858309/attention-spans-goldfish/.

7. Grabowski, David. "A Slot Machine in Every Pocket."
   Medium. Hyperlink Magazine, May 17, 2018. https://
   medium.com/hyperlink-mag/a-slot-machine-in-every-
   pocket-4f12d7ae116c.

8. October, Heidi, David Sarro, Isabella January, and Adrian
   Lim February. "Understanding Cell Phone Addiction."
   PsychAlive, March 2, 2017. Accessed November 13, 2019.
   https://www.psychalive.org/cell-phone-addiction/.

9. "Signs and Symptoms of Cell Phone Addiction."
   PsychGuides.com. Accessed November 13, 2019. https://
   www.psychguides.com/behavioral-disorders/cell-phone-
   addiction/signs-and-symptoms/.

10. "Teenage Drug Addiction: Why They Use Harmful
    Substances – Rehab Spot." RehabSpot. Accessed
    November 13, 2019. https://www.rehabspot.com/drugs/
    who-addiction-affects/teenage-drug-addiction/.

11. "Teen Drug Abuse – Signs of Teenage Drug Use –
    Addiction Center." AddictionCenter. Accessed November
    13, 2019. https://www.addictioncenter.com/teenage-
    drug-abuse/.

12. Suburbanstats.org. "Current Richmond, Kentucky
    Population, Demographics and Stats in 2019, 2018."
    SuburbanStats.org. Accessed August 18, 2019. https://
    suburbanstats.org/population/kentucky/how-many-
    people-live-in-richmond.

Chapter 12: Dodging the Comparison Trap

1. "Comparing Quotes (28 Quotes)." Goodreads. Goodreads. Accessed December 21, 2019. https://www.goodreads.com/quotes/tag/comparing.

2. "Depression Higher in Rich Countries, Study Suggests." LiveScience. Purch. Accessed November 18, 2019. https://www.livescience.com/35792-global-depression-rates.html.

3. "Lots of Time on Social Media Linked to Anxiety, Depression in Teens." U.S. News & World Report. U.S. News & World Report. Accessed November 18, 2019. https://www.usnews.com/news/health-news/articles/2019-09-11/lots-of-time-on-social-media-linked-to-anxiety-depression-in-teens.

Chapter 13: Overcoming Sin

1. "Billy Graham Quotes." BrainyQuote. Xplore. Accessed December 10, 2019. https://www.brainyquote.com/authors/billy-graham-quotes.

Chapter 14: Finding Godly Influences

1. "Show Me Your Friends and I'll Show You Your Future – By: Chaplain Ronnie Melancon." thibodauxpd, November 21, 2013. https://thibodauxpd.wordpress.com/2013/11/24/show-me-your-friends-and-ill-show-you-your-future/.

2. "Home." Go to Investing, Raising Capital, Sales Training, and Recruiting with Social Media. Accessed December 26, 2019. https://www.thevirtualhandshake.com/2004/09/14/a-reason-a-season-a-lifetime-but-who-is-michelle-ventor/.

3. Habeeb Akande Quotes (Author of Illuminating the Darkness).” Goodreads. Goodreads. Accessed December 26, 2019. https://www.goodreads.com/author/quotes/6437294. Habeeb_Akande.

4. “A Quote by Oprah Winfrey.” Goodreads. Goodreads. Accessed December 26, 2019. https://www.goodreads.com/quotes/4602-everyone-wants-to-ride-with-you-in-the-limo-but.

5. “Ben Shapiro Quotes (Author of The Right Side of History) (Page 4 of 8).” Goodreads. Goodreads. Accessed December 26, 2019. https://www.goodreads.com/author/quotes/255605.Ben_Shapiro?page=4.

6. Peterson, Jordan B., Ethan Van Sciver, and Norman Doidge. *12 Rules for Life: an Antidote to Chaos.* Toronto: Vintage Canada, 2020.

PART 3: LAND

Chapter 15: Leaving Your Imprint

1. “New Cigna Study Reveals Loneliness at Epidemic Levels in America.” Cigna, a Global Health Insurance and Health Service Company. Accessed August 3, 2019. https://www.cigna.com/newsroom/news-releases/2018/new-cigna-study-reveals-loneliness-at-epidemic-levels-in-america.

2. “Inky Johnson - Some People Don’t Need You to Preach a...” Facebook Watch. Accessed December 22, 2019. https://www.facebook.com/watch/?v=700548160409666.

3. “A Quote by Albert Einstein.” Goodreads. Goodreads. Accessed July 29, 2019. https://www.goodreads.com/quotes/84604-setting-an-example-is-not-the-main-means-of-influencing.

4. Goleman, Daniel. "Long-Married Couples Do Look Alike, Study Finds." The New York Times. The New York Times, August 11, 1987. https://www.nytimes.com/1987/08/11/science/long-married-couples-do-look-alike-study-finds.html.

5. Smith, Colin. "God Can Restore Your Lost Years." The Gospel Coalition. The Gospel Coalition, March 20, 2019. https://www.thegospelcoalition.org/article/god-can-restor-your-lost-years/.

6. "I Wanted to Change the World." A Gift of Inspiration. Accessed June 29, 2019. http://www.agiftofinspiration.com.au/stories/personalgrowth/Change.shtml.

Chapter 16: Fulfilling Your Dreams

1. Gilbert, Sara. "How the Law of Diminishing Intent Nearly Killed My Business." Forbes. Forbes Magazine, December 13, 2017. Accessed August 19, 2019. https://www.forbes.com/sites/forbescoachescouncil/2017/02/10/how-the-law-of-diminishing-intent-nearly-killed-my-business/#35f6f48e7347.

2. "A Quote by Anonymous." Goodreads. Goodreads. Accessed January 2, 2020. https://www.goodreads.com/quotes/7842132-if-you-don-t-sacrifice-for-what-you-want-what-you.

3. Elk, Kathleen. "How David Goggins Went from an Exterminator Living Paycheck-to-Paycheck to a Navy SEAL." CNBC. CNBC, May 15, 2019. https://www.cnbc.com/2019/05/15/how-david-goggins-went-from-broke-exterminator-to-navy-seal.html.

4. Moore, Anthony. "Why Most People Will Remain in Mediocrity." Medium. Mission.org, January 31, 2019. https://medium.com/the-mission/why-most-people-will-remain-in-mediocrity-6c7e24c48d12.

5. YouTube. YouTube. Accessed September 8, 2019. https:// www.youtube.com/watch?v=LZeSZFYCNRw.

6. Matthew Stone, Joi-marie Mckenzie. "Jennifer Lawrence OK after Both Engines Failed on Private Plane, Rep Says." ABC News. ABC News Network, June 11, 2017. https://abcnews.go.com/Entertainment/ jennifer-lawrence-private-plane-forced-make-emergency-landing/story?id=47968911.

7. "A Quote by Les Brown." Goodreads. Goodreads. Accessed October 6, 2019. https://www.goodreads.com/quotes/884 712-the-graveyard-is-the-richest-place-on-earth-because-it.

Chapter 17: Facing Failure

1. ZamTheWriter. "Microsoft Exists Because Paul Allen and Bill Gates Launched This High School Business First." CNBC. CNBC, October 16, 2018. Accessed November 15, 2019. https://www.cnbc.com/2018/10/16/microsoft-exists-because-paul-allen-and-bill-gates-launched-this-high-school-business.html.

2. "Albert Einstein Biography." Encyclopedia of World Biography. Accessed November 15, 2019. https://www. notablebiographies.com/Du-Fi/Einstein-Albert.html.

3. Pak, Eudie. "Walt Disney's Rocky Road to Success." Biography.com. A&E Networks Television, June 27, 2019. Accessed November 15, 2019. https://www.biography.com/ news/walt-disney-failures.

4. Hendry, Erica R. "7 Epic Fails Brought to You by the Genius Mind of Thomas Edison." Smithsonian.com. Smithsonian Institution, November 20, 2013. Accessed November 15, 2019. https://www.smithsonianmag.com/ innovation/7-epic-fails-brought-to-you-by-the-genius-mind-of-thomas-edison-180947786/.

Chapter 18: Escaping the Comfort Zone

1. Marinoff, Evelyn. "Why the Comfort Zone Is Not That Bad After All." Medium. The Startup, February 11, 2019. https://medium.com/swlh/why-the-comfort-zone-is-not-that-bad-after-all-121904ae9bb0.

2. "Twenty Years, 20 Firsts -- Shaun White Lands First McTwist 1260, Scores First Snowboard SuperPipe Three-Peat." X Games. Accessed December 1, 2019. http://www.xgames.com/events/2014/austin/article/10921544/twenty-years-20-firsts-shaun-white-lands-first-mctwist-1260-scores-first-snowboard-superpipe-three-peat.

3. "A Quote by Master Oogway." Goodreads. Goodreads. Accessed September 9, 2019. https://www.goodreads.com/quotes/2212546-yesterday-is-history-tomorrow-is-a-mystery-and-today-is.

4. "Rocky Balboa Quotes by Sylvester Stallone." Goodreads. Goodreads. Accessed December 4, 2019. https://www.goodreads.com/work/quotes/10446115-rocky-balboa.

5. "A Quote by Muhammad Ali." Goodreads. Goodreads. Accessed December 4, 2019. https://www.goodreads.com/quotes/1445903-i-don-t-count-my-sit-ups-i-only-start-counting-when.

6. "Brian Tracy Quotes (Author of Eat That Frog!)." Goodreads. Goodreads. Accessed December 4, 2019. https://www.goodreads.com/author/quotes/22033.Brian_Tracy.

7. Fahkry, Tony. "Why the Magic Happens When You Step Out Of Your Comfort Zone." Medium. Mission.org, January 1, 2018. https://medium.com/the-mission/why-the-magic-happens-when-you-step-out-of-your-comfort-zone-8698ccfbfc6a.

8. Blackboxfilmcompany. YouTube. YouTube. Accessed December 4, 2019. https://www.youtube.com/user/blackboxfilmcompany/videos.

Chapter 19: Walking it Out

1. "Elon Musk Quotes (Author of Elon Musk)." Goodreads. Goodreads. Accessed December 1, 2019. https://www.goodreads.com/author/quotes/7221234.Elon_Musk.

2. Goodwin, Lindsey. "How Much Is Starbucks Coffee in Countries Around the World?" The Spruce Eats. The Spruce Eats, August 18, 2019. https://www.thespruceeats.com/how-much-is-starbucks-coffee-766065.

3. Admin. "Why Is Gas Mileage Different in the City and on the Highway?" Lexington Toyota, July 26, 2017. https://www.lexingtontoyota.com/blog/gas-mileage-different-city-highway/.

ACKNOWLEDGEMENTS

This book wouldn't have been possible without many people around me. I must first thank God for guiding me and giving me the inspiration and words to write.

Next, to my terrific teachers and coaches: I wouldn't have many of the ideas and experiences to write about without your positive influences. You all have encouraged me more than you'll ever know!

I'm grateful for the Kentucky Christian Writer's Conference, which prompted me to make my dream a reality.

The team with Author Academy Elite publishing have been amazing to work with, and the coaching calls with Kary Oberbrunner kept my momentum going. You've surely ignited this soul!

Additionally, I must give a huge shout out to Nanette O'Neal and Felicity Fox, my remarkable editing team with The Guild. The finesse you've added to my book is brilliance.

Lastly, all the encouragement from my family and friends have refueled me in the times when I was discouraged, tired, and tempted to quit. Throughout it all, you never stopped believing in me.

... And for that, I thank you.

ABOUT THE AUTHOR

Noah Halloran is a sixteen-year-old emerging influencer with a message that unveils masks and refines authenticity in today's teens. Calling young people forth into who they're created to be, he's trailblazing a path towards clarity in a confusing world, and, as a torchbearer, he offers guidance to those who've lost their direction. Noah is a dedicated student striving for excellence in the classroom, in character, and in serving his community. He has a passion for distance running and resides in Kentucky with his mom, dad, and younger brother, Elijah.

AUTHOR ACADEMY elite

LET'S CONNECT!

Follow Noah Halloran on Social Media

 Instagram.com/Noah.Halloran

 Facebook.com/Noah.Halloran.Author

Twitter.com/NoahHalloran1

Made in the USA
Monee, IL
07 July 2020

36103235R00128